Toxic people can drain our lives, rob us of our joy, and worse. Unfortunately, many of us don't have the skills to address these individuals in the best way possible. We know we are to love, forgive, and be patient, but those aren't God's only solutions. Gary Thomas has done a masterful job of showing us how and when to confront in the right way, how to guard one's heart, and, most importantly, when to walk away. His comprehensive treatment of the many times Jesus chose to leave a person or a situation provides overwhelming encouragement in learning to love well, truth well, and behave well. Highly recommended.

John Townsend, PhD, *New York Times* bestselling author
of the *Boundaries* series and *People Fuel*, founder of the
Townsend Institute for Leadership and Counseling

Gary Thomas has done it again. He's given us a biblically grounded pathway toward healthy living—especially in our relationships. In *When to Walk Away*, he provides the steps we all need in managing toxic people and high-maintenance relationships. It's encouraging, practical, and desperately needed. Don't miss out on this life-changing message.

Drs. Les and Leslie Parrott, authors of
Saving Your Marriage Before It Starts

This book is a must-read. There is no more confusing or pressing question for many of us than this one, and Gary Thomas brilliantly, sensitively, and pastorally gives us a path forward. I'm grateful for this book, and I'll be buying ten copies and handing them out to many!

Jefferson Bethke, *New York Times* bestselling author
of *Jesus > Religion* and *To Hell with the Hustle*

Toxic relationships leave us bewildered and drained, and we all experience them, some closer to home than others. If you are wondering what to do next and unsure of what God has to say, Gary Thomas has written this practical and helpful book for you.

Jennie Allen, author of *Nothing to Prove* and
founder and visionary of IF:Gathering

Grace and forgiveness are critical components of the Christian life. But the Bible also offers instruction for those times and situations when we encounter people who are so destructive—to individuals and to the work of God's kingdom—that our wisest course of action is to just "walk away." Gary Thomas offers solid, biblical counsel for those who are grappling with the destructive influence of a toxic person.

Jim Daly, president of Focus on the Family

Toxic people can be a powerful and destructive force that can create a great deal of harm. As a mental health specialist, I appreciate the carefully crafted wisdom in these pages. You will find biblical truth backed by specific strategies to keep yourself healthy and prevent you from becoming a victim of controlling behavior. I highly recommend *When to Walk Away.* You will find relief and hope in these pages.

Gregory L. Jantz, PhD, CEDS, founder
of The Center • A Place of HOPE

Although we are called to love unconditionally, God does not require us to persevere in relationships that are toxic, dangerous, and soul crushing. This is especially good news for individuals in destructive marriages. The chapter on toxic marriage is so helpful, not just for suffering individuals, but for well-meaning people who often misapply biblical passages to encourage those in toxic marriages to keep enduring for Jesus. God does not value the sanctity of marriage more than the safety and sanity of the people in it.

Leslie Vernick, speaker, relationship coach, and bestselling
author of *The Emotionally Destructive Relationship*

As a Christian woman, I'm often too worried about being nice. Gary Thomas shows us that it's not about doing what others want but what God wants. Don't let someone else derail God's purpose for you! As Gary says, sometimes you have to walk away from something to walk toward what God really wants.

Sheila Wray Gregoire, marriage and sex blogger
at ToLoveHonorandVacuum.com

WHEN TO TO WALK AWAY

FINDING FREEDOM FROM TOXIC PEOPLE

GARY THOMAS

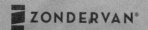

ZONDERVAN

When to Walk Away
Copyright © 2019 by The Center for Evangelical Spirituality

Requests for information should be addressed to:
Zondervan, *3900 Sparks Dr. SE, Grand Rapids, Michigan 49546*

ISBN 978-0-310-34676-0 (hardcover)

ISBN 978-0-310-34681-4 (international trade paper edition)

ISBN 978-0-310-35599-1 (audio)

ISBN 978-0-310-34679-1 (ebook)

Published in association with Yates & Yates, www.yates2.com.

Cover photo: katherinegregorio / Shutterstock
Interior design: Kait Lamphere

Printed in the United States of America

19 20 21 22 23 24 25 26 /LSC/ 15 14 13 12 11 10 9 8 7 6 5 4 3 2

"There is a friend who sticks closer than a brother."
PROVERBS 18:24

When you're writing about toxic relationships,
you're reminded of the healthy relationships
that help keep you grounded, especially in ministry.
God has graciously provided
several ministry-oriented "brothers in arms"
who have with their wisdom and experience
helped me pursue God's best in life and ministry.
It is to these four men I dedicate this book:
Dr. Mike Dittman, Dr. Steve Wilke,
Mike Woodruff, and Kevin Harney—
and no, Steve, these names aren't listed
in any significant order, so don't take any offense.

CONTENTS

CHAPTER 1

A MOST CLEVER ATTACK

Greg was sorely confused.

His coworker Aaron claimed to be a Christian, yet he seemed to relish attacking others. Aaron specialized in creating offensive nicknames for coworkers and others outside the office. He policed the entire office, even people who didn't report to him, making sure they adhered to a policy he had lobbied to get passed. Aaron was a master sleuth at uncovering personal secrets and launching them into a juicy gossip chain. He blatantly lied about coworkers' words and actions to pit one person against another so he could play both sides as a "comforting defender."

One coworker had enough of this and called him out on it, and Aaron convinced the boss to lay her off, which created a terrifying wall of protection against anyone else who thought about standing up to him.

While Aaron was toxic toward everyone in the office, he put on a different face with the boss. He had convinced his boss that he was the one true loyal employee and that everyone else was out to get him. He also used a twisted sense of humor to become the boss's favorite lunch mate.

Greg felt paralyzed because the toxic work environment impacted his physical health, his mental state, his family life, and his sleep. He needed the job, but Aaron was making his workplace torturous. It was so bad that Greg admitted he couldn't leave Aaron at the office. Mentally, Aaron followed him home and haunted him at night. Greg dreaded driving into work in the morning. His wife or one of his children would start talking to him in the evening, and he found himself tuning them out, mentally back in the office, second-guessing what he had said or done, trying to figure out a way to make sense of what felt like a crazy situation.

"Why does Aaron want to control everything?" Greg asked me. "How can he get any joy out of acting like that? What pleasure is there in spreading gossip about everyone else, lying to make people hate each other? And how can he call himself a Christian when he makes everybody else's life feel like a living hell?"

Sadly, the only role I could offer Greg was as an empathetic but naive listener. Back then, I had no understanding of how to handle toxic people. I'm sure I'd be ashamed of the pious advice I gave him about setting an example, praying for Aaron, turning the other cheek, etc.

It wasn't until I found myself in the crosshairs of similar toxic personalities that I realized toxic individuals feed off misunderstood piety and are *enabled* by false Christian guilt to spread their attacks far and wide.

This naïveté of mine carried on for decades. Much later in life, I was caught off guard when, at first, a woman seemed pleased that I was speaking out on an issue she felt had been too long ignored in the church. She wrote to me to thank me, and then suggested I read her book and another person's book to get even more information.

I was honest with her and made no promises. This was a one-time blog post, I explained. Addressing this issue wasn't a primary calling in my life, so I couldn't promise to read two entire books on the topic. It wasn't anything personal; it was just a matter of time.

She was greatly offended and then launched a vicious attack.

No longer was I a friend; I was an enemy. In fact, I had helped cause the problem I was trying to address, and even my blog post, which seemed to agree with her, was only a cover for my ignorance and own evil behavior. And people should read and buy her book while demanding that my books be pulled from publication.

I spent way too much time, lost too much focus, and expended too much energy trying to placate a toxic person. My desire is to encourage, lift up, and support others through my writing and speaking. Here's where my ignorance brought much distraction and angst. For most of my adult life, I've focused only on playing offense when it comes to ministry. No one taught me about playing spiritual defense. The very idea seemed "unchristian."

I'm not speaking here about "professional" ministry, by the way; I'm referring to every believer's call to spread God's love and truth to people wherever we live and work, whether it's in a bank or a bakery or on the ballfield. God's work will be attacked in many very clever ways. If we fail to learn how to play defense, we're going to be tied in knots of false guilt and distraction. As we are sidetracked, fewer people will be loved and served, and we'll bring unnecessary misery into our lives.

I used to think, *If I can just become a little holier, a little wiser, more loving, a little more patient, a bit more knowledgeable about the Bible, more surrendered to the Holy Spirit, etc., then everyone will "see Jesus" in me and line up to hear what God has to say.* When someone didn't respond or became hostile, I thought, *Is there compromise in my life holding me back? Are my words lacking grace? Did I not hear God correctly?*

So I spoke and wrote almost exclusively about playing offense.

When writing about marriage and parenting, I stressed playing a good offense: love, serve, sacrifice, and cherish. I didn't stress enough the need (sadly) for some couples and individuals to play a little defense.

It wasn't until a friend of mind, Dr. Steve Wilke, noticed my distress as I endured another toxic attack that he began to teach me about the need to occasionally play defense.

"Gary," he said, "read the book of Luke. Jesus walked away from people many, many times."

Dr. Wilke's passing remark opened my eyes to an entirely new dimension of ministry: *defense.* With new eyes, I saw how Jesus *frequently* walked away from intended persecution. I read how Paul, Peter, and even the "apostle of love," John, warned early believers to beware of certain toxic individuals. It's wise and loving to focus on playing offense, but to play offense without any defense is to make ourselves unnecessarily vulnerable and severely diminish our impact.

My lack of defense, my naïveté in thinking that a stellar offense makes a good defense unnecessary, held me back for thirty years of adult ministry. I have wasted way too much time on toxic people, and not one of those toxic people came out the better for it. But many reliable people whom I could have interacted with were ignored or given less attention so I could devote my time trying to placate the malignant.

I'm done with that. I repent of that.

I want to play the best offense possible: Know the Word inside and out. Surrender to the Holy Spirit's guidance. Live in the affirmation of the Father and the grace of the Son. Love others sacrificially and enthusiastically.

But I believe future years of ministry can be even more fruitful if I learn to also play a little defense along the way.

If you've never been a people pleaser, this may all seem rather elementary. If you find it easy to write people off, you may justifiably say, "Welcome to the world of being an adult, Gary." But if, like me, you've let guilt and misplaced "compassion" tie you up in knots as you tried to figure out why a relationship or ministry situation made you feel like you've lost your mind, you may find this book to be very helpful.

I got a call from Greg a few years back. He hadn't talked to or seen Aaron in fifteen years until Aaron tracked him down by email and warned him he needed to hire a lawyer. Aaron said he was going to sue him. (For the record, Aaron never actually filed a lawsuit.)

If you have any doubt whether toxic people exist and typically refuse to cede control or give up their attacks, just ask around.

There are certain people who drain us, demean us, and distract us from other healthy relationships. Long after they're gone, we're still fighting with them in our minds and trying to get them out of our hearts. They keep us awake. They steal our joy. They demolish our peace. They make us (if we're honest with ourselves) weaker spiritually. They even invade times of worship and pervert them into seasons of fretting.

They are toxic, and we know they are toxic, but perhaps they're a lifelong friend, relative, or coworker. You can't avoid all troublesome people, can you? And aren't we supposed to reach difficult people? Didn't Jesus tell us to search for sinners?

And so we keep engaging them, keep running into a wall, all the while thinking we're doing the Lord's work.

But what if we're not?

What if there's another way of looking at how we handle toxic people in our lives? What if the way and work of Christ are so compelling, so urgent, and so important that allowing ourselves to become bogged down by toxic people is an offense to God rather than a service to God?

Toxic has become a psychological catchphrase of the day, but you'll see how steeped in Scripture this approach is. In fact, I quote more Scripture in this book than in any of my previous books. This truth about playing defense was staring me in the face the dozens of times I read the Bible; I was just too blind to see it. The mere act of Jesus letting so many walk away has changed the way I look at life, ministry, and service.

A Clever Attack

If someone is getting in the way of you becoming the person God created you to be or frustrating the work God has called you to do, for you that person is toxic. It's not selfish for you to want to be who God created you to be, and it's not selfish for you to do what God created you to do, so it's important to learn how to be on the lookout for toxic people. That may mean cutting them out of your life when possible or severely limiting your exposure to them when there's no better solution.

One of the cleverest attacks against God's church today centers around our guilt in dealing with toxic people. Satan knows he can't stop God's people from loving and caring, because God's Spirit makes us love and care. What he can do, however, is urge us to pour most of our God-breathed love, intention, and goodwill on people who actually resent it and who will never respond to grace. Satan can't stop God's clear water from flowing through us, but he *can* tempt us to pour it straight into the gutter, quenching the thirst of no one and creating no fruit.

This trap needs to be exposed, and God's people need to be set free.

One caveat before we begin. Some use the label *toxic* much too broadly as an excuse to avoid difficult, different, or hurting people. Let's not do that. As we'll see in chapters 3–5, *toxic* has a special designation that we can learn to discern and then manage accordingly. Yet there are naive Christians who aren't on the lookout for any toxicity and who then find themselves going crazy because they become overwhelmed by something for which they have little understanding and no label.

There are perhaps far fewer truly "toxic" people than we may think, but the reason we need an entire book to address them is that their negative assaults are inordinately effective. In the wise words of the seventh-century monk John Climacus, "A single wolf, helped by a demon, can trouble an entire flock."[1] In more contemporary language, one toxic person can all but empty a solid midsize church if he or she isn't called out on it.

Toxic people ruin family gatherings. They assault friendships. They can run businesses into the ground. While their numbers may be relatively small, their influence, unfortunately, is not. They murder ministries. They rob saints of their joy and peace and sometimes make us question our sanity.

It's time to call them out. It's time to make the most of the one life God gives us, and that means we have to learn how to play a little defense. Resolve today that the toxic people won't take you down or even distract you. Your mission matters too much for that.

Road Map

Here's where we're going to go and what we're going to discuss. The entire book hinges on studying the life of Jesus, who walked away from others (or let others walk away from him) many times. Understanding his methods of playing defense will inform how we preserve our call to love and serve (playing offense). We'll look closely at how Jesus played defense in chapter 2.

Chapters 3–5 will define what a toxic person is. Toxic people can be toxic in different ways, but we'll show some of the major markers.

Then—this is so key—chapters 6 and 7 ("No Time to Waste" and "Reliable People") lay out the case for focusing on playing offense. Matthew 6:33 and 2 Timothy 2:2 tell us how crucial it is to be active servants and what we are to focus on in our service. This book is about protecting our mission from toxic attacks even more than it's about protecting ourselves from toxic people.

Chapter 8 explores Jesus' famous passage where he warns us not to throw pearls to pigs. Chapter 9 looks at the difference between labeling and name-calling; if it seems harsh to you to call someone "toxic," you'll find this chapter particularly helpful. Chapter 10, "A Man with a Mission," uses Nehemiah as a particularly excellent example of someone who kept their mission on point in the face of many toxic attacks.

Since it's not always possible to walk away from toxic people, chapter 11 explores how to "look like Jesus when working with Judas," and chapter 12 follows up by teaching the sad but essential reality that in order to maintain our mission before God, we must learn how to be hated without letting it distract or destroy us.

Chapter 13 offers a biblical view on how evil infects every good thing that God has created on this planet. That sets us up for chapter 14, where Jesus tells us that our allegiance to his spiritual family takes precedence over our allegiance to our blood family of origin. Chapter 15 helps us sidestep the common (and vicious) attack leveled by family members: "How come you're not acting like a Christian?"

Chapters 16–19 apply all we've been learning to family relationships with our parents, spouses, and children. Chapter 20 gives a powerful example of a man who learned to leave his toxic ways behind, and chapter 21 teaches us to be less toxic toward ourselves. The epilogue speaks a final pastoral word to those who have been harmed by toxic behavior.

I had envisioned that this would be a short book, about half of what it has become. Once I opened up the Scriptures, however, it was like the glaciers melted and the dams overflowed, and I had to ride the rivers way downstream.

I hope you enjoy and learn from the ride.

Takeaways

- Because toxic individuals exist, we need to learn how to play defense. Focusing only on offense is naive and undercuts the impact we can have with others.
- Seeing Jesus walk away from others or let others walk away from him presents a model to consider in our own lives.
- Toxic individuals drain us of joy, energy, and peace.
- One of Satan's cleverest attacks is getting us to pour our time and energy into people who resent the grace we share and who will never change, keeping us from spending time with and focusing on others whom we can love and serve.
- There may not be a lot of toxic people numerically, but they tend to have an inordinately negative effect on families, churches, relationships, and ministries, so we need to be on the lookout.

CHAPTER 2

WALKAWAY JESUS

Since Jesus came from heaven to walk among us, Christians tend to think that walking away from anyone, or letting anyone walk away from the truth, is a failure on our part.

But Jesus walked away or let others walk away . . . a *lot*.

After my conversation with Dr. Wilke, I reread the gospels and counted every occurrence where Jesus deliberately parted ways with others. Sometimes he spoke a hard truth, after which the other person walked away. Other times, the people had been touched and begged Jesus to stay, but he had other places to go and left them. Overall, I counted forty-one such instances in all four gospels.[1] Forty-one! Some of these references refer to the same encounter, but that still leaves more than two dozen distinct times when Jesus demonstrated walking away or letting someone else walk away.

These occurrences weren't always rooted in conflict. Sometimes Jesus walked away from others who wanted more of him. On still other occasions, he retreated for his own refreshment and renewal or protection. The point is that Jesus didn't let the needs, pleas, attacks, or unresponsiveness of others distract him from the mission given to him by his heavenly Father.

One thing we don't see when others walk away is Jesus giving chase. As powerful as Jesus was, as brilliant as Jesus was, as pure as Jesus was, and as surrendered to God as Jesus was, not everyone he interacted with "changed," repented, or agreed with him. Here's the principle that comes from that: *Sometimes to follow in the footsteps of Jesus is to walk away from others or to let them walk away from us.*

---

1. See appendix ("Jesus Walking Away").

Take, for instance, the story of the rich young ruler. Jesus discerned this young man's heart and the core issue in his life—he loved money. When the earnest young man couldn't walk away from his money, he chose to walk away from Jesus. Notice that our Lord didn't run after him. Jesus didn't say, "Wait! I know asking you to give 100 percent is a bit extreme; if you give away just 50 percent, I think we can make this work. I need followers! Let's bargain!"

No, he turned to his disciples (*reliable people*[2]) and explained what had just happened and why it was so difficult for that rich man to join them. This is a direct example of Jesus choosing to spend time training reliable people rather than spending more time with a closed person. "Toxic" doesn't seem to fit this young man's profile, but the principle is clear: when truth is rejected, spend your time on those who will receive it instead of begging closed-hearted people to reconsider.

On another occasion, after giving a difficult teaching about eating his flesh and drinking his blood, Jesus lost a *lot* of previously enthusiastic followers: "From this time many of his disciples turned back and no longer followed him. 'You do not want to leave too, do you?' Jesus asked the Twelve" (John 6:66–67).

Notice the same pattern. Not just one, but *many* walked away. And not just casual onlookers; they're called his "disciples." Instead of chasing them down and begging them not to misunderstand him and to please come back, Jesus turns to the reliable people, the Twelve, and says, "So, what about you?"

Notice the confidence that gives authority to his message. Jesus never appears desperate, manipulative, or controlling, as if when people didn't agree with him, his feelings would be hurt. He is mission-focused and others-centered to his deepest core.

Jesus also demonstrates the need to sometimes "verbally" walk away when dealing with a toxic person, like Herod. Instead of arguing with Herod and trying to justify himself, Jesus remained silent:

---

2. You'll read the phrase "reliable people" several times before I explain its spiritual significance in chapter 7, when we discuss 2 Timothy 2:2.

"[Herod] plied him with many questions, but Jesus gave him no answer" (Luke 23:9).

Jesus adopted the same approach with Pilate and the religious leaders: "When he was accused by the chief priests and the elders, he gave no answer. Then Pilate asked him, 'Don't you hear the testimony they are bringing against you?' But Jesus made no reply, not even to a single charge—to the great amazement of the governor" (Matthew 27:12–14).

We don't have to argue. When a toxic person is attacking you, you don't have to participate. Especially when you know it won't make any difference, spend those few moments worshiping and relating to your loving heavenly Father rather than contending with a hateful assault.

A particularly vivid example of Jesus letting someone walk away occurred at the Last Supper. Jesus knew Judas was going to betray him. He spoke about it in advance. And yet he allowed Judas to walk out of the room. He didn't chase after him. He didn't waste time trying to change Judas's mind. Instead, he spent every last minute he had left investing in his faithful, reliable disciples and in prayer right up until the moment he was arrested.

Many plastic bracelets have been sold with the words "What Would Jesus Do?" If you're dealing with toxic people, you may want to get a bracelet that reads, "What Would Jesus *Not* Do?"

The answer is, "He wouldn't chase after them."

Please Leave

One of the most painful passages for me to read in Scripture occurs after Jesus demonstrates his power to a city by sending an entire herd of pigs tumbling over a cliff.

Having been visited by Jesus, these farmers were among the most blessed people in the history of the world by getting to hear God speak in the flesh. When Jesus got in the way of their pig farming, though, the loss of their business blinded them to the glory of the person standing in front of them. In a crude sense, this town chose pork chops over salvation: "Then the whole town went out to meet Jesus. And when they saw him, they pleaded with him to leave their region" (Matthew 8:34).

Can you imagine an entire town looking at Jesus—the Messiah we love, the one we wish we could talk to *face-to-face*, the one we'd pay a year's salary to get a personal audience with for one hour—and pleading with him to *leave*?

And yet Jesus didn't argue. We're told that "Jesus stepped into a boat, crossed over and came to his own town" (Matthew 9:1).

He walked (or in this case sailed) away.

There's a terrible messianic complex in many of us that thinks if we were more intelligent or a little holier, if we fasted and prayed a bit more, then everyone we shared the truth with would agree with us and welcome God into their hearts.

That didn't happen for the *real* Messiah, and it certainly won't happen for us. It's okay to walk away when people resist the truth. And it's okay to let them walk away.

It took a while for Jesus' followers to get this. They often remained more enamored with the people's response than Jesus' truth. For example, when Jesus challenged the way the Pharisees put human tradition over the commands of God, the disciples "warned" him, "Do you know that the Pharisees were offended when they heard this?" (Matthew 15:12).

Listen to Jesus' response: "Every plant that my heavenly Father has not planted will be pulled up by the roots. *Leave them*; they are blind guides" (Matthew 15:13–14, emphasis added).

Leave them.

You don't always have to stay and argue with unreasonable people who are offended by truth.

Turn Away

Some of you still can't imagine turning someone away or letting someone walk away, even if the relationship has become toxic. Your Lord and Savior doesn't have that problem: "Many will say to me on

20

that day, 'Lord, Lord, did we not prophesy in your name and in your name drive out demons and in your name perform many miracles?' Then I will tell them plainly, 'I never knew you. Away from me, you evildoers!'" (Matthew 7:22–23).

Jesus actually *sends* these people away. He spoke the truth and respected people's choices. As we'll discover in a later chapter, controlling others is a primary sign of toxicity, not a method for ministry. Jesus never cheapened the beauty of what he was saying by appearing desperate. In fact, he pretty much took the opposite approach: *This is what's true; take it or leave it.* That confidence built the early church.

Lord of His Life

Jesus didn't just walk away from toxic people; he was also willing to walk away for purposes of ministry effectiveness and strategy. He never allowed the desire of others to dictate who he spent his time with. After a powerful time of ministry, Jesus became a rock star of sorts, and hordes of people wanted to be around him. Jesus had gotten up early in the morning to pray, but the disciples furiously tracked him down and said, "Everyone is looking for you!"

Listen to Jesus' reply: "Let us go somewhere else—to the nearby villages—so I can preach there also. That is why I have come" (Mark 1:38).

Just when people most wanted him to stay, Jesus often left: "When Jesus saw the crowd around him, he gave orders to cross to the other side of the lake" (Matthew 8:18).

Jesus wasn't moved by either standing ovations or jeering ridicule. He was truly Lord of his life. Neither should we allow the neediness of others or the toxicity of others to determine where, when, and how we spend our time. Neediness can be a subtle form of toxicity. Our spiritual radar goes way up when someone forcefully attacks us, but a passive-aggressive neediness can slip in unawares and steal our attention even more effectively than a full-frontal assault.

If someone is trying to control you, that itself is toxic. Whether they use force or guilt, direct attack or unreasonable neediness ("You're the only one who can help me, and you have to help me *now*"), it's still all about control. Controlling someone (or letting yourself be controlled) is wrong.

An experienced pastor once pointed out to me that Jesus chose his disciples, and so should we: "Jesus went up on a mountainside and called to him those he wanted, and they came to him. He appointed twelve that they might be with him" (Mark 3:13–14).

Jesus didn't just model this mastery of his calendar; he specifically taught his disciples to do likewise:

> "If anyone will not welcome you or listen to your words, leave that home or town and shake the dust off your feet."
>
> MATTHEW 10:14

> "When you are persecuted in one place, flee to another."
>
> MATTHEW 10:23

Jesus didn't tell his disciples, "Stay there and let them hit you because they may finally come to their senses." No. He gives his disciples permission—even more than that, a command—to flee from those hurting them and go to another place. (If you're wondering, *What about when he said to turn the other cheek?* see the endnote.)[1]

For added balance, sometimes Jesus walked away, not to accomplish more ministry, but to recharge: "Yet the news about him spread all the more, so that crowds of people came to hear him and to be healed of their sicknesses. But Jesus *often* withdrew to lonely places and prayed" (Luke 5:15–16, emphasis added).

If we try to minister when our own fuel tanks are empty, we may end up doing more harm than good. We should follow Jesus' example and not feel guilty about telling others no until we have first sat at the feet of our heavenly Father and received his love and care. We have to occasionally play defense in order to go back on the offense with renewed passion and fervor.

As far as allowing himself to be mistreated, though Jesus came to die the death of a martyr, *he didn't allow consistent and persistent abuse to continue throughout his life*. He let himself be tortured and crucified *once*, but there were many occasions before that when he "slipped away" from those who wanted to hurt him.

Here are just three examples from the gospel of John:

> At this, they picked up stones to stone him, but Jesus hid himself, slipping away from the temple grounds.
>
> JOHN 8:59

> Again they tried to seize him, but he escaped their grasp. Then Jesus went back across the Jordan to the place where John had been baptizing in the early days.
>
> JOHN 10:39–40

> So from that day on they plotted to take his life. Therefore Jesus no longer moved about publicly among the people of Judea. Instead he withdrew to a region near the wilderness, to a village called Ephraim, where he stayed with his disciples.
>
> JOHN 11:53–54

And here's one from Matthew:

> But the Pharisees went out and plotted how they might kill Jesus. Aware of this, Jesus withdrew from that place.
>
> MATTHEW 12:14–15

Your persecution may not be physical stoning, but emotional shaming, slander, gaslighting, etc.[3] Jesus once entered a ruler's house

---

3. "Gaslighting" is a term used to describe someone who tries to defend their own reprehensible behavior by making you feel crazy for calling them out on it.

to heal a dead girl. Notice the juxtaposition of how the people responded and what happens next: "They laughed at him. *After the crowd had been put outside*, he went in and took the girl by the hand, and she got up" (Matthew 9:24–25, emphasis added).

Jesus didn't argue with the crowd. He also didn't just stand there and take it. He had the crowd "put outside."

And *then* he did his work.

In the course of kingdom work, whether you're serving God in an office, at a soccer field, or in a school, being abused is inevitable. It seems to me that for every Christian who is bent on seeking first the kingdom of God, there is a corresponding number of Christians bent on telling those seeking first the kingdom of God that they are seeking the kingdom in the wrong way. We can't avoid this pushback without leaving this planet, but we can learn to walk away when the time is right and as God leads (which is what this book seeks to teach you). We can "put those people outside" and carry on our work.

Here's what I'm getting at: don't think that letting yourself be abused is always the holy choice. Proverbs 22:3 reads, "The prudent see danger *and take refuge*, but the simple keep going and pay the penalty" (emphasis added). The teacher is telling you it is supremely *wise* to step aside in the face of danger. If you don't, you may pay a penalty, but *not* because of your "obedience." Rather, your pain will be caused by being "simple."

If life is about following Jesus, then at times we will follow him as he walked away from abuse and danger. Jesus didn't cede control of his life to anyone. He told his disciples that his death would be *his* choice, not his enemies': "The reason my Father loves me is that I lay down my life—only to take it up again. No one takes it from me, but I lay it down of my own accord. I have authority to lay it down and authority to take it up again" (John 10:17–18).

So then, in his words and in his practice, Jesus modeled how to let people go, how to walk away, and how to stay in charge of our

---

They deny what you know to be true, attempting to make you feel confused and shamed so you'll drop the issue.

schedule (and to a certain degree, not allow ourselves to be unnecessarily abused). Follow in the footsteps of Jesus by boldly walking away and finding a reliable person in whose life you can make a worthy investment (see chapter 7).

We've got an entire book left to explore how to apply this. How do we know when to walk away? How do we find the balance between playing a good offense and an appropriate defense?

Before we get to all that, let's take a few chapters to more clearly define what we're talking about when we use the word *toxic*.

Takeaways

- Jesus walked away from others (or let others walk away from him) more than two dozen times in the four gospels.
- At times, Jesus remained verbally silent when others tried to goad him into a conversation or a foolish controversy.
- When people asked Jesus to leave, he usually complied.
- Not only does Jesus let others walk away; at the great judgment he will *send* people away. You won't be able to reach or influence everyone you meet.
- Sometimes Jesus walked away for personal refreshment, prayer, or the need to reach others.
- Though Jesus came to die the death of a martyr, he repeatedly walked away from persecution, attacks, and violence throughout his adult ministry. In the same way, it can be prudent for us to walk away from verbal, emotional, or physical abuse.

CHAPTER 3

A MURDEROUS SPIRIT

Toxic people aren't just difficult people. They're not "unsaved" people. They're not merely unpleasant people. The toxic people we're talking about in this book are the kind of people who are basically taking you down and destroying your mission. They deflate your enthusiasm and make you feel like you're going crazy (thus making you feel like you have nothing to say to others), and they are masters at eliciting shame, guilt, and discouragement.

The challenge is that there's no one exhaustive definition of a toxic person. Certain traits are common: They are often ruled by selfishness and spite. They are usually draining instead of encouraging, and they use people instead of loving them. They are often seemingly addicted to self-righteous, rash judgments and thus frequently fight with people instead of enjoying and appreciating people. They may be jealous of healthy people's peace, family, and friendships and spend much of their time and effort trying to bring people down to their level of misery rather than blessing others with joy and encouragement. They often want to control you, and it may feel as if they *just want you to stop being you*.

The next three chapters will explore three common elements of toxic opposition. Not every toxic person will exhibit all three, but every toxic person usually excels in at least one: a murderous spirit, a controlling nature, and a heart that loves hate. This chapter will focus on the "murderous spirit."

I want to make it clear that I'm not saying we should avoid "sinners." We are all sinners, and we are to reach out to sinners. Toxicity is something else. Toxic people exist inside and outside the church and are those trying to *take you down*. A thirty-minute interaction with them (in person, on the phone, or even in a Facebook exchange) can require a week of recovery. You keep thinking about what they said, and you're so disturbed you can't get them out of your mind. You find yourself fighting with them even when they aren't present, and they keep showing up in your thoughts even when you're not trying to go there.

Listen, you know that's not a healthy reaction. You know fretting about someone isn't part of the abundant life. Choosing to walk away means recognizing that your faith doesn't necessarily call you to put up with that.

A Wrecked Year

Roommates Andrea and Grace came back from class one day to find another person in their room. Their school had assigned Samantha to their suite, and that single decision to add another student to their suite in effect cost Andrea her first year in college.

Andrea and Grace soon learned that Samantha needed to have a beef with someone in order to get out of bed. It was something Andrea or Grace had done, to which both readily apologized for being so thoughtless. Or not done, to which both apologized for being so insensitive. Then she ranted almost every day over something someone else had done or not done. Andrea noticed that Samantha had experienced more conflict in her first two weeks at university than Andrea had experienced in the first two decades of her life.

If Andrea and Grace went to a meal alone, Samantha made them pay with a lecture about how selfish they were. If they wanted to study when Samantha needed to blow off steam about how someone had disrespected her so rudely earlier in the day, they both got lectures about putting work before people—and, after all, how would Jesus look at that?

Andrea grew up in a polite Christian home where you were taught to get along with everybody. She is a self-described people pleaser who places a high value on being nice. "I can't stand it if someone is angry with me," she confesses. And so she went out of her way to placate Samantha's fierce anger, and Samantha zeroed in on this vulnerability. Because Andrea was more willing to engage Samantha than Grace was, she unwittingly made Samantha's attacks more "fun," so Samantha focused the brunt of her intensity on Andrea (though never entirely leaving Grace alone).

In spite of Andrea's good intentions, Samantha went out of her way to irritate her. Knowing Andrea liked her things put in an orderly manner, Samantha rearranged everything in their shared spaces and bathroom. Andrea and Grace explained that Samantha could put her things where she wanted them, but could she please not move theirs?

Samantha stomped out of the room, slammed the door, and then—to show how deeply offended she was that her idiot roommates didn't appreciate her hard work on their behalf—went next door, knowing the thin walls muted nothing, and told the neighbors how badly Andrea and Grace had treated her.

Andrea tried to reconcile. She's an earnest Christian believer, and she'd never had a relationship quite like this. She was quick to apologize and take responsibility for sins she probably hadn't committed. Samantha picked up on this weakness and made it her personal agenda to fix Andrea's "issues." She knew a counselor she often spoke to from her hometown, so she went over everything with the counselor on the phone and came back to Andrea with her idea for healing and reconciliation: "He's pretty sure you have some demons in you, but if you'll go visit him with me, he'll drive them out."

Andrea explained that wasn't something she was willing to do, which only further convinced Samantha how deeply troubled and mired in evil Andrea truly was. What kind of sick person willingly harbors demons when someone is offering to drive them out?

Andrea's skin began breaking out, which feels like a big deal in your first few months of college. Her calls home were prolonged and tearful, and she started staying out late and getting up very early to avoid being around Samantha. Of course, that meant Andrea was perpetually tired, nodding off in class and acting listless around her friends.

She talked to her Resident Adviser, who saw this as just two young people needing to learn how to get along and offered a few platitudes about Christian forgiveness, patience, humility, and grace. Bolstered by her mom, who was by this time understandably concerned about Andrea's health and well-being, Andrea eventually went above the RA and received a transfer from the room after the Thanksgiving vacation.

Grace was at first upset with Andrea for abandoning her to live alone with Samantha (toxic people tend to be masters at turning people against each other), but now that Andrea was gone, Samantha turned her full firepower on Grace. Grace was out of the room by Christmas.

The RAs randomly assigned another student to the suite, and that person begged to be out of there by Easter.

Holidays seemed unkind to Samantha.

Andrea's RA finally realized it wasn't a matter of offering a few platitudes about getting along. Samantha was a truly toxic person, and she needed to be treated accordingly.

My own college years were formative. Some of the deepest friendships I've ever known were forged and maintained during that season. It was a fruitful time of Christian discipleship, and I dated and married my wife during those four years. If ever there was a season I'd want to be fully alive, it would be during college, but Andrea lost her first year of school trying to deal with and then escape Samantha's toxicity. Samantha all but murdered it.

In fact, even today, several years later, if you bring up Samantha's name to Andrea, in her own words, "I still get that feeling in my gut that instantly makes me want to hurl." Andrea regrets that because she was so focused on Samantha she missed out on meeting a lot of new people. When she agreed to bring Samantha along with her, others sensed Samantha's toxicity almost immediately and began judging Andrea: "If that's who Andrea likes to hang with, it's best to move on."

Andrea wanted to help Samantha fit in, but of course she was unsuccessful. You can't bring a wild wolverine into a preschool and hope the enthusiasm and gullibility of the kids will placate the vicious nature of the wolverine.

It sounded so "unchristian" to Andrea to think about cutting Samantha off—Jesus says to love the unlovable, right? But sacrificing herself didn't help Samantha at all, and it hurt Andrea's first year significantly.

That's been my experience with toxic individuals. I've never helped one of them; I've just lost tons of time and focus trying to make sense of crazy.

Here's how I look at it now: I'm not a medical doctor. If someone has a broken arm, I can call a physician for them and show some empathy, but it would be irresponsible to think I could heal them. That kind of assistance is above my training and experience, and I'm likely to just make things worse if I get overly involved. When someone is a truly toxic individual, most of us normal people will be in over our heads. You can try all you want, but thinking you can be the one who breaks through is more likely to humble you than to change them.

You don't have to believe me; life alone will teach you, if you let it.

Toxic people murder. They murder relationships, turning people against each other. They murder churches, turning meeting times into gigantic fights instead of worship and service. They murder workplaces, destroying productivity. They murder reputations. They will seem to kill your joy and peace and even threaten your sanity.

My "toxicity radar" goes off whenever I sense that a person or group of persons seems to exist primarily to take another person or organization down. The New Testament's method, based on the nature of God, is demonstrating God's beauty and excellence and persuading others by word and example, often with seemingly miraculous tolerance and always with the hope of redemption. Satan's modus operandi is silencing and murdering with shame, ridicule, and malice, with no grace and no redemption. Ever.

I've seen many people claim to do God's work while seeming to use Satan's methods.

A Murderous Spirit

Our Creator God gives life and breathes life. Wherever there is life, God is somewhere behind its genesis. He had some impact, some influence, something to do with that creation.[1]

Jesus spoke of Satan as a murderer (John 8:44) who is obsessed with death. Murder is more than wanting someone's lungs to stop breathing; there is the murder of ministry, the murder of reputation, the murder of happiness, and the murder of peace. In Matthew 5:21–22, Jesus expands the definition of murder to include malicious intent.

When you disagree with a person who has done evil, he or she often won't just disagree with you and let it go. Some will hate you to the point of murder, merely for pointing out their sin: "For John had been saying to Herod, 'It is not lawful for you to have your brother's wife.' So Herodias nursed a grudge against John *and wanted to kill him*" (Mark 6:18–19, emphasis added).

It's not enough for a toxic person to say, "You and I will have to agree to disagree." If your beliefs make them feel guilty, they want to remove your voice and influence, even if that means removing . . . *you*.

We see a similar spirit to Herod's unleashed today, with large swaths of people who don't think Christians who hold certain views (many of which the church has held for most of its history) should be able to voice their opinions. They want them to disappear or to be completely silenced. They will use shame or the law, but they will be vicious nonetheless.

The best label for this silencing is social murder.

Healthy people can disagree and walk away. Toxic people harbor a murderous spirit, at least in the sense of wanting to completely discredit you and *shut you up*. The apostle John warned, "Anyone who hates a brother or sister is a murderer, and you know that no murderer has eternal life residing in him" (1 John 3:15).

---

1. John 1:3–4: "Through [Jesus] all things were made; without him nothing was made that has been made. In him was life, and that life was the light of all mankind."

When you read the book of Acts, the story of the early church is the story of opponents using every means—the law, persecution, ridicule, shaming, name-calling, and often physical murder—to get them to shut up. Some of the early church's opponents were motivated by genuine religious disagreement. Some were motivated by the loss of income (like when a fortune-telling slave girl was delivered of her "gift" by Paul and Silas in Acts 16:16–18.). Sometimes it looks like demonic opposition. But the end goal of this toxicity was always the same: *Stop! Be silent. Kill what you're doing and saying, or we'll kill you.*

Murdering a Ministry

Alex was forty years old when he had his first affair. His wife, Alice, forgave him and said she wanted to work on their marriage. She supported him as he climbed up the administrative ladder in his company, even relocating when he got a promotion (which meant Alice had to restart her own counseling practice). She figured that getting away from the "scene of the crime" could help bring their family back together.

A decade passed, during which Alice suffered the effects of a narcissistic husband. In spite of the affair, Alex expected Alice to speak of him in private and public as the greatest husband who ever lived. When their church asked Alex to consider becoming a deacon (though they had no ministry request for Alice), she gently questioned him: "They don't know about the affair, do they?"

"How long are you going to hold that over my head?" Alex asked. "You're never going to truly forgive me, are you?"

His confidence was charismatic, so Alice was often told how lucky she was. Alex overheard these comments and would bring them up persistently: "You realize how many other women wish their husbands were more like me?"

Alex's hobbies governed weekends and vacations, and his work schedule commanded most weeknights. Alice rescheduled appointments and did her best to accommodate Alex's lavish spending by cutting back on her own wardrobe, which is why it hurt a bit more when she saw what one of her husband's coworkers wore at an office party. She could see Alex's eyes drinking in the beauty of his colleague, and the corresponding deadness when he turned his attention back to her, as if she was an annoyance for being by his side.

She had already lived through this once and tried to gently bring it up. "Alex," she said, "if someone sees the two of you together, it's not going to look like a business relationship."

Alex was so offended and angry that Alice knew—she just *knew*—that it *wasn't* just a business relationship.

"I forgave you once," she said, "but I won't put up with this again."

Alex's company and church wouldn't look kindly on an affair and a divorce, so Alex set about convincing people how much of a living hell it was being married to Alice. He asked pastors for "help" with his negative wife who was likely suffering from a mental illness. She had to be mentally ill if she didn't realize how fortunate she was to be married to him.

Alice knew where this was headed: the only way Alex could divorce her and marry his coworker and maintain his standing with his company and church was to murder Alice's reputation. He laid the groundwork by mastering the art of "asking for prayer." She found out he had been giving "updates" about her "condition" and how she was doing.

When a sufficient amount of time passed, he "reluctantly" filed for divorce. Within months, he openly "thanked God" for the comfort of his female coworker (the same one who wore that beautiful dress at the party) who was helping him through this crisis.

Dr. M. Scott Peck warns that toxic people love to scapegoat and blame others for the chaos they create: "A predominant characteristic . . . of the behavior of those I call evil is scapegoating. Because in their hearts they consider themselves above reproach, they must lash out at anyone who does reproach them. They sacrifice others to preserve their self-image of perfection."[1]

Scapegoating is another word for murder: "I want *you* to take the fall for *my* sins." Alex felt threatened by a spiritually healthy wife who wouldn't lie to him or for him anymore. He left the woman who had shown him such grace and predictably began to spread vile lies about her, suggesting *she* was the evil one who was perhaps not even mentally balanced and certainly not fit for ministry.

Peck again: "It is characteristic of those who are evil to judge others as evil. Unable to acknowledge their own imperfections, they must explain away their flaws by blaming others."[2]

Evil is a harsh and dangerous word, but what else would you call a man who wrongs a woman deeply, a woman who has been used by God and is gifted by God to bring deep healing and discerning clarity to others, and still he seeks to destroy her ministry by spreading lies about her and casting aspersions on her character? Alex defends himself by attacking Alice: "I cheated on her and abandoned her, so you should too. Otherwise I might feel guilty about what I've done and have to face the awful truth about how toxic I've become."

Just as Alex murdered Alice's self-esteem by cheating on her twice; just as he murdered her vocation by always insisting she follow him and start her own ministry from scratch whenever anything better turned up for him in another city; just as he murdered Alice's social calendar by demanding that she cancel whatever she had scheduled to accommodate his late-breaking appointments; just as he murdered her children's home by pursuing a divorce—now he sought to murder her ministry to justify his affair and abandonment.

As we'll see in a future chapter, the importance of properly addressing toxic people is necessitated in large part so we can preserve our mission before God. Jesus asked us to pray that God would send *more* workers into the vineyard, so for a supposed "fellow believer" to try to destroy another worker's work is about as evil as it gets.

I grieve for the families who may not hear Alice's wise words, the church members who may not hear her future teaching, the families who may not receive her pastoral care, *all so that a narcissistic, adulterous man can justify filing for divorce and a quick remarriage.*

It gets worse, unfortunately. This dear sister in Christ was ground up by members of the church, since she was "tainted" by divorce. "How can she bring healing to other families if her own family was ripped apart?" they asked. Such simplistic thinking played right into her toxic husband's plans. That's exactly how he wanted people to think: "It's too risky, so it's best to avoid her."

The only reason Alex succeeded (in a limited sense) is because a naive and uninformed church cooperated with him. If I were a senior pastor who refused to hire Alice primarily because she was divorced, I would be an accessory to the murder of her ministry.

When Alex remarried, he posted "happy" pictures of the ceremony on Facebook, describing his new wife as "Mrs. Alex Doe." It's like he had digitally murdered Alice and "replaced" her, *using her former name*. This was a digital dagger intended to hurt.

Alex's three children were old enough to be appalled at what he had done to their mother, so there was some understandable alienation. When he got engaged soon after the divorce was final, he eventually forced a meeting with his oldest daughter. He had not seen or talked to her in more than a year, but rather than asking for her forgiveness or inquiring about her welfare, he justified all that he had done and was doing by pointing out its effect on *him*: "Don't I look good? I haven't been this healthy and happy or looked this good in years, have I? Aren't you happy for me?"

Happy that her family had been murdered?

Happy that her mother had been cheated on and her ministry assaulted?

Happy that he found such great joy while not seeing his own daughter for more than twelve months?

Happy?

Seriously?

But that's the way toxic people think. A murderous spirit destroys every last vestige of empathy until they become a self-absorbed wrecking ball. Others must pay the price for their happiness.

Life!

When Paul exorcised a foul spirit, keeping a fortune-telling slave girl in captivity, the girl's owners stirred up the crowd, brought Paul and Silas before the political authorities, and beat them up.

Notice that Paul's kindness—freeing the soul of an oppressed woman, freeing a *slave* girl, is met with a murderous response. Her owners not only brought political charges and sought to generate religious opposition, but they stripped Paul and Silas (murdering their dignity), put them in prison (murdering their freedom), and beat them up (murdering their health).

Murder, murder, murder . . . all because Paul had done something good and holy and just.

But here's where the story gets amazing and hopeful and so moving you'll want to worship God for half an hour.

It's midnight.

Paul and Silas are in "the inner cell" of the prison, their feet fastened in stocks. They are praying and singing hymns to God while the other prisoners are listening. In this place of darkness and death, they are bringing light and life.

There's an earthquake and *all* the prison doors are opened and *everybody's* chains break loose—not just Paul's and Silas's (Acts 16:23–28).

The jailer wakes up, sees what has happened, and draws his sword to kill himself. The Romans would kill him for letting this happen, and it wouldn't be a pleasant death.

This is the man who unjustly held Paul in prison for doing a good thing, a holy thing, a kind thing. Yes, the guard was a tool of other oppressors, but he was, at the very least, a cooperating tool. Paul might be tempted to think he was about to get what he deserved.

Yet what does Paul do? He cries out, "Don't harm yourself! We are all here!" (Acts 16:28).

God's people always want the murdering to end.

Paul tells the jailor and other prisoners how they can find salvation—life!—and the jailor brings Paul to his family, where all then are saved: "He was filled with joy because he had come to believe in God—he and his whole household" (Acts 16:34).

In a world filled with murderous intent, we are privileged and blessed to be people who bring joy, light, life, and hope. We don't silence; we persuade. We resist murder and live to bring salvation.

Reading about murderous people has the potential to engender hatred and murder in your own heart. Let's be like Paul and Silas—in the midst of others who seek to murder us, let's pray and worship and keep our eyes fixed on the God of creation and life so that we live to bring salvation and hope.

In resisting toxic people and acknowledging them, never let yourself become like them. The beauty of life in Christ isn't built or enhanced by a negative reaction to evil; it's cultivated and maintained by responding to the beauty of who God is.

Takeaways

- Toxic people aren't just "difficult" or "sinful" people. They display certain characteristics.
- One brand of toxicity is best described as a murderous spirit. The characteristics of a murderous spirit are:
  - consistently creating chaos in other relationships
  - being known for what they are against more than what they are for
  - being unwilling to simply disagree with you, but wanting to silence you
  - attempting to stop you from doing or being what God has called you to do or be
  - sapping your strength and assaulting your health
  - scapegoating you and others so their own sin won't look so bad
- Jesus and the early church frequently confronted such a murderous spirit, and we can expect that we will have to as well.
- Like Paul and Silas, we should respond to murderous intent by being people who seek to bring life and salvation.

CHAPTER 4

CONTROL MONGERS

Barry reached out to me when his wife, Rachel, said she wanted a divorce. Rachel told me why she wanted to end the marriage: every part of her life was being controlled.

"He's a sweet man, but he's an engineer and needs to control *everything*."

"Give me an example."

"I can give you a dozen. We have to eat at Mexican restaurants six days a week. He won't let me cook at home, and I'm so sick of Mexican food I can hardly stand it.

"We have to go to church on Saturday night, never on Sunday morning. When it comes to sex, it's every Wednesday night, in a certain position on the side of the bed with a towel underneath me, before we go out for Mexican food and then church.

"I'm his concierge. From morning till night, all that matters is his work and schedule. If we watch television, it has to be sports—no Hallmark or HGTV, ever. If I get sick, he's angry that I can't serve him and he'll leave me alone. His weekend schedule is so rigid—when we wake up, when he works out, when and where we eat—that I can't make any plans of my own. The only social contacts we have are the waiters at his favorite Mexican restaurant. I'm suffocating, and I just can't keep living this way."

And then the kicker: "He started to doubt me, even though I've been completely faithful. He put a tracker on my phone and makes me account for every second of my day."

I'll spare you the other details, but there were more examples.

Barry sat quietly without defending himself. That actually impressed me a bit.

"Is all this true, Barry?" I asked.

"Everything she told you is 100 percent true."

Barry never saw this as "controlling" behavior. Instead, he just considered himself as "hardheaded or, from a positive standpoint, resolute and convinced. When you're an engineer, you need to get things right. And if the system works, why change it?"

Rachel felt like she was suffocating. She had divorce papers drawn up but not served.

In this instance, I felt like a separation was their only hope—for Rachel to catch her breath and for Barry to feel the gravity of his actions. Rachel already had rented an apartment, but I told Barry, "You caused this, and if you want to fix it, you need to let Rachel stay in the house and you go live in the apartment."

He gulped, but he wanted to save his marriage, so he did.

Even more difficult, I told him that all control was over. "You can't contact Rachel unless she contacts you. She needs a break. Even a text with a Bible message will feel like you're squeezing her. If she calls you, talk all you want. If she texts you, you can text back. But don't show up at the house and don't reach out to her until she's ready."

As a man used to controlling everything, Barry looks back and says, "To this day, doing what you told me to do was the hardest thing I've ever done in my life."

I asked Rachel to wait before serving Barry the divorce papers. "I will never ask you to go back to being controlled like that," I assured her. "But I'm asking you to consider whether you'd be willing to go back to a different marriage and a different Barry. He has confessed what he's done. He is willing to make this right. Can you give him that chance?"

Rachel loved Barry. You've heard the negative, but there are many sweet characteristics that she treasures—his wit, his warmth, his love for God.

Rachel agreed to wait, but I didn't ask her to "tear up the papers," not just yet. I thought Barry needed to know those papers were sitting in an office drawer ready to be pulled out at any time, because it wasn't going to be easy for him to make such major changes.

I later told Barry privately that he'd know his heart had changed when he wouldn't want Rachel to come back to him if that meant she'd be controlled. "Love is about wanting what's best for your wife, above and beyond what you want for yourself. When you get to the point where you can say, 'I'm afraid for Rachel to come back until I know I've changed,' then your marriage can be rebuilt."

They walked out of my office to their separate cars, and Barry said to Rachel, "Well, maybe we should go out and have coffee and discuss what Gary told us."

Rachel looked at him. "Did you not hear what Gary said? I'm getting in my car and leaving."

Rachel needed to do this. She needed to breathe. And Barry, as much as it hurt, needed to let her go.

Barry needed to learn that controlling behavior is *toxic behavior*.

The God Who Lets Us Choose

As powerful as God is and as sovereign as God is, he is never controlling. His loving call and invitation to his people, in both the Old and New Testaments, is based on *choice*. One of the most famous passages in the Old Testament is Joshua's declaration to Israel: "*Choose* for yourselves this day whom you will serve" (Joshua 24:15, emphasis added).

Joshua learned this from his mentor Moses, who said, "This day I call the heavens and the earth as witnesses against you that I have set before you life and death, blessings and curses. Now choose life, so that you and your children may live and that you may love the LORD your God, listen to his voice, and hold fast to him" (Deuteronomy 30:19–20).

In the New Testament, consider Galatians 5:13 ("You, my brothers and sisters, were called to be free. But do not use your freedom to indulge the flesh"), John 7:17 ("Anyone who chooses to do the will of God will find out whether my teaching comes from God or whether I speak on my own"), and, of course, Revelation 3:20 ("Here I am! I stand at the door and knock. If anyone hears my voice and opens the door, I will come in and eat with that person, and they with me").

As we read in a prior chapter, Jesus seems startlingly *not* controlling throughout his earthly ministry, letting people walk away or walking away himself dozens of times. Jesus—God in flesh—spoke the truth and allowed people to respond as they chose.

But do you really want to know how *not* controlling God is? He allows Satan and demons to continue their nefarious ways. Two somewhat obscure passages (Isaiah 14; Revelation 12) have led many scholars to speculate (it's not particularly clear) that perhaps one-third of the angels rebelled against God to follow Satan. The Bible doesn't give us the details, and we won't gain much from speculating about the origin of the dispute. If we needed to know more, the Bible would tell us more.

But isn't it fascinating that God, whom we know *could* shut them down, *doesn't*? We know he will, but for the present time, God allows Satan to make his case and to even deceive and lure people away.

God proclaims his truth, sends his messengers, and even offers grace for willing hearts to receive it, but he doesn't possess anyone. The New Testament talks about demon-possession, but it never talks about God-possession.[1] While God's Spirit moves us, inspires us, fills us, and equips us, the apostle Paul is adamant: "The spirits of prophets are subject to the control of prophets" (1 Corinthians 14:32). If we were "possessed" by the Holy Spirit in the same way we speak of demonic possession, we would not be warned to avoid grieving the Spirit (Ephesians 4:30). The possibility of being able to grieve the Spirit necessitates that we are still in control enough to do so.

C. S. Lewis describes this demonic bent toward "possession" in harrowing terms when the demon Screwtape explains, "With beasts the absorption takes the form of eating; for us [demons], it means the sucking of will and freedom out of a weaker self into a stronger."[1]

---

1. Demon-possession or some form thereof is mentioned in Matthew 9:32–33; 12:22; 17:18; Mark 5:1–20; 7:26; and Luke 4:33–36, among other places. For those wondering about 1 Peter 2:9, where the Greek *eis peripoiēsin* is sometimes translated as "God's possession," the context is clearly about God accepting someone as his own, not God controlling someone in the way that demonic possession is most commonly understood. *Possession* here is a noun, not a verb. I accept my son and daughters as "my own." I don't try to invade their minds or control their actions.

One of the evils of addiction is that we gradually lose control. Self-control is listed as a fruit of the Spirit. Addiction—the lack of control—is a fruit born in hell.

God respects us as he made us and invites us to the highest life possible, but he will allow us to reject him and suffer the consequences.

In the interest of theological precision, let me add that God goes far beyond persuasion. He does impact history; he has done and still does perform miracles; and he is involved in hardening and softening hearts. But the Bible presents this as part of our interaction with God. God hardened Pharaoh's heart (Exodus 7:3), but we're also told that Pharaoh hardened his own heart (Exodus 8:15). I'm not trying to construct a full theology of God here. While God does determine events as well as persuade, his nature leads us to conclude that for humans to control other humans is a toxic act rather than a reflection of who God is and who God calls us to be.

Sovereignty and Free Will

If you grew up with a view of God who controls everything, you probably grew up in a tradition that taught the proper doctrine of the sovereignty of God without equally explaining our responsibility.

Calvinists (who typically focus on God's sovereignty and deny free will) and non-Calvinists will approach this topic differently, but neither, properly understood, speak of God as coercing anyone. John Calvin himself wrote that "we allow that man has choice and that it is self-determined, so that if he does anything evil, it should be imputed to him and to his own voluntary choosing. We do away with coercion and force, because this contradicts the nature of the will and cannot coexist with it."[2] While believing that our wills are hampered, Calvin adds, "It makes a great difference whether the bondage is voluntary or coerced. We locate the necessity to sin precisely in corruption of the will, from which follows that it is self-determined."[3]

Calvinists and non-Calvinists may disagree on whether it's proper to use the phrase "free will," but both agree that no matter how God's sovereignty is understood and exercised, sovereignty and the claim of ultimate authority are *God's alone* to exercise. We are decidedly not God, *so humans attempting to control other humans is a blasphemous assumption of authority and worship that should be directed only to God.*

That's why dictatorships are evil. It's why slavery is an abomination. There are certain circumstances—prohibiting dependent children from certain behaviors, imprisoning those who are violent (based on the choices they've made to hurt people)—where exercised authority is appropriate, but even while certain restrictions are granted, full-on control is evil.

The highest human life is a life surrendered to God above everyone and all things. When I want anyone to focus on pleasing *me*, I am acting like an anti-God—the antichrist, if you will. I am asking them to respond to me like they should respond only to God.

If Jesus modeled walking away rather than exerting controlling behavior, how can we act any differently?

Popular author, speaker, and pastor Jack Deere discovered a painful truth when he realized his wife was an alcoholic. When his pleas failed to "change" her, he tried to control her. Looking back with admirable humility, he admits his error: "I had told my wife that she had to choose sobriety for herself and then tried to force her to make that choice. I had treated her like a child and then expected her to make decisions like an adult."[4]

God doesn't "control" us, even in our sin; we cannot and must not try to control one another. When a husband is trying to control a wife or a wife is trying to control a husband; when a "leader" is controlling an organization instead of empowering it; when a child uses rebellion and violence to take over family gatherings; when a colleague gossips, slanders, and sows division so that he or she can rule the office, you know you're dealing with a toxic person.

Whenever we start to control someone, we're stepping away from God's image toward toxicity, the favored purview of Satan. God-inspired ministry proclaims truth courageously while respecting others' choices. Whenever you hear of manipulation and control, you often suspect a cult, not a true expression of Christian faith.

Looking back, Rachel believes she allowed Barry's controlling behavior to go on for so long because there were many other things she loved about him. And other wives seemed to have it worse. "Barry never hit me. He wasn't verbally abusive. Except for the controlling nature, he really is a sweet man."

By putting up with the hypercontrol, however, Rachel understandably reached a breaking point. Freed from his presence during the separation, she felt like she could breathe again. They worked out a system where if Rachel texted Barry a heart emoji, he was free to text back. Barry lived for those hearts.

In a very short period of time, Rachel started to miss him. "I remembered his loving and tender ways," she said. "He was my best friend; we could talk about anything. I missed that companionship. Not hearing from him or seeing him made me want him more. I was just afraid that, like an alcoholic going back to the bottle, if we immediately got back together, the controlling behavior would start all over again."

For Barry, the separation was "awful and so lonely. I felt helpless, weighed down by a mountain of regrets, and with so much time alone on my hands, those regrets finally turned into repentance and reconciliation with Jesus. I lay in bed and repented for all the things Rachel had rightfully accused me of. For three hours in the middle of the night, I cried my heart out to Jesus."

Exhausted, Barry heard the Lord speak into his heart: "My son, you're forgiven. I love you."

"I fell back in love with Jesus. I knew my life was going to be different, but I knew I had zero credibility with Rachel, and I didn't know how that would turn out."

As Rachel's heart softened, Barry got another heart emoji. It was like a drug that woke him up. He jumped to attention and texted a quick paragraph, and then his heart leaped when he saw the flickering dot, dot, dot that told him she was responding.

Then the dots died, as did his heart.

Rachel was still cautious.

They started spending time together again at my suggestion, with Rachel arriving in a separate car so she could leave whenever she wanted to. "Barry seemed like a different person," Rachel remembers, "but I wasn't sure it would last. He was so sweet and loving, but that's how he was when we first started dating. Yet I could tell that something was *different* about him. He got everything right with Jesus. He was softer toward God, a broken man. A man like that is going to act differently in marriage."

Barry spent weeks sitting in his rocking chair after work in a small apartment, reading his Bible and studying. He didn't watch any secular television. Though he had a past history with pornography, now it wasn't even a temptation. God seemed to fill the room, and he lost his taste for what used to be his crutch when times got difficult.

Many weeks passed. Rachel gradually let the visits become more frequent. And then, when she invited him back home, Barry felt like an infatuated teenager. More importantly, he backed it up with actions.

Rachel glows now. "Since we've been back together, I've never made the bed again; I've never been to the grocery store again. When my car gets to a quarter of a tank, Barry fills it up with gas. He buys roses every Saturday when he goes to the grocery store. And when I went on a mission trip to Uganda, he sent me a *picture* of flowers on Saturday."

The same methodical nature that Barry previously used to control Rachel he now employs to serve and bless her.

Just going to Uganda was a change for Rachel. Five years ago, Barry wouldn't have "allowed" it.

Barry admits, "I hate even the thought of saying I wouldn't *allow* it, as if I had to *let* her go, but that's what our marriage used to be like. Now we talk about it. It's such a different marriage."

Barry not only likes his marriage; he likes himself more: "I'm a controller. Rachel is really good about helping me when I slip back into controlling behavior. It's up to me to fix it and stop it. If you keep close to Jesus, he'll help you."

Rachel seemed so beaten down when she first came to my church office that when she returned a couple months later, some of the people barely recognized her. There was new life, new joy, and a new beauty. She actually looked like a different person. Enduring toxic behavior can squeeze the life out of someone, and it's not to be trifled with or minimized. But now, a couple years later, Rachel is an exuberant person.

"Everything about the marriage is better," she says. "Sexual intimacy is absolutely the best. We've enjoyed lots of different things. I have more peace, and I feel more complete. My love for Barry has grown more than I ever thought it would. I've seen the change Jesus made in him. It's been a couple of years, so it's proven how he walks the walk and talks the talk now. He's also changed in his relationships with other people. He supports me in my own real estate business in a way he never did before."

They both point out, however, that controlling behavior will always be a temptation for Barry. Rachel has to call him out on it at times, and Barry, to his credit, maintains a humble and repentant heart.

As a gentle reminder for where they once were, Rachel will occasionally send Barry a single heart emoji. When she really wants to excite him, she'll send him a text with dozens of hearts in a row.

Toxic control just about killed their marriage, but Jesus saved it.

Being controlled makes you feel like you're living in hell. Loving in freedom is the closest a couple gets to heaven on this side of eternity.

Takeaways

- In the Old and New Testaments, God reveals himself as a God who respects and allows choice.
- Extreme control, like demonic possession, is something Satan employs; it's not God's mode of operation.
- One human trying to control another is a toxic act of evil.
- Our focus should be on inspiring others to give their highest allegiance to God, not on living to please us or agree with us.
- Getting rid of Barry's control issues ushered Barry and Rachel into a new and much richer season of marriage.

CHAPTER 5

LOVING HATE

I am among the minority of people who are hardwired (genetic science now demonstrates this) to loathe cilantro.

I can't stand it.

I call it the adolescent of herbs: notice me, *notice me, NOTICE ME!*

To my taste buds, a little bit of cilantro can wreck an entire meal. I don't believe God makes any mistakes, but I do believe this world would be a better place if cilantro had never been used as seasoning, because so many chefs, especially those who make salsa (which I *love*), seem to think cilantro makes almost everything taste better.

Yet many people, in fact *most* people, are genetically wired to enjoy cilantro. I don't get it. I'll never get it. But if you're one of those people, please don't offer to cook for me.

In the same way, as Christians, we are spiritually wired for compassion, kindness, humility, gentleness, patience, and love (Colossians 3:12, 14). Those qualities should be delicious to us. They should feel like they "fit" us when we put them on. We should respect them, desire them, and feel most alive when we exhibit them. It's a good day if we demonstrated compassion, displayed kindness, walked in humility, treated others with gentleness and patience, and took the opportunity to love others as much as was possible.

There's another spiritual makeup, unfortunately, that has an entirely different kind of taste. This particular brand of toxic person feels most comfortable when they exhibit anger, rage, malice, slander, filthy language, and lying (Colossians 3:8–9). We don't get how some people seem to "come alive" when they are most malicious, murdering someone's reputation, saying awful things, and deceiving people. We just don't get it. But toxic people do. It's their "cilantro."

Standing Up to Toxicity

Jonathan Byrd is a five-time winner on the PGA tour. He plays with a number of different men every weekend, so he's run across more than his share of "personalities." One fellow golfer, whom we'll call "Golfer X," was notorious for his temper and biting remarks that assaulted volunteers, fans, caddies, fellow players, and marshals. He was, in fact, filled with rage, anger, and malice, and he unleashed plenty of filthy language. He was the walking bad example of Colossians 3:8–9.

Jonathan has one of the most pleasant personalities I've ever come across. He's one of those genuinely likable guys, and he values the role of volunteers. "Volunteers aren't professionals," he explained to me. "Most of them work one tournament a year. If we had to pay our volunteers, our purses would be cut in half. They're so valuable to the tour, but golfers can get very fickle"—and sometimes even toxic.

Jonathan and Golfer X were playing in a final round on Sunday. Neither were going to win or even place highly in the tournament. It was more a case of finishing out the round and flying home.

That seemed to put Golfer X in his worst mood. He snarled at fans and volunteers alike.

On the fifth hole, Golfer X and Jonathan walked up to a blind tee shot. You couldn't see the hole, or even the second half of the fairway. Golfer X teed up his ball and started taking practice swings.

The marshal, somewhat apologetically, said, "Mr. X, the group in front of you is still in the fairway."

Golfer X sneered at the marshal and mocked him by saying, "No . . ., Sherlock."

The marshal backed away. "I'm sorry," he said, "I was just trying to help."

Jonathan had had enough. "Apologize to him."

"Apologize for *what*?"

"For being a jerk [to be honest, he didn't actually say "jerk"]. He was just doing his job."

There was a long, uncomfortable silence. When Golfer X was

cleared to play, he hit a slice forty yards out of bounds and played out the hole with a double bogey.

"What happened for the rest of the round?" I asked Jonathan, laughing.

"We played the next thirteen holes in complete silence."

The thing is, Golfer X was also silent toward everyone else. He just stewed in his own toxicity but didn't verbally harass anyone else the rest of the day, so Jonathan's confrontation may have made one guy angry, but it spared many others.

What I like about what Jonathan did is that he used his influence and position—a fellow professional—to protect those who were more vulnerable, namely, volunteers. If a marshal gets into a fight with a player, he's going to lose (except maybe at Augusta). Jonathan decided that he'd use his platform to make the world a little less toxic for the fans and volunteers.

In your own workplace, if you work "under" a toxic person, your options may be limited to walking away or learning how to not let what they do bother you. Some people just seem to love hating others. But people who have influence over toxic people are the ones who need to rise up and take a protective role.

Understanding Those Who Love to Hate

Longtime counselor Dan Allender and biblical scholar Tremper Longman III help us understand the spiritual makeup of people who love hate. They bring up a distinction about motivations that I've found to be very helpful. Writing almost thirty years ago, Allender and Longman use the word *evil* instead of *toxic*, but we're essentially discussing the same thing: "Evil is devoid of conscience. It lacks moral boundaries; right is whatever it desires. A seared conscience does not respond with mercy to a cry for help, nor is it stopped by the threat of shame."[1]

This is important. *If you employ "normal" methods of resolving conflict with a toxic person, they won't work.* Toxic people don't respond to empathy, and they're not afraid of shame. They have different motivations and different fears than "average" people.

If you tell a toxic boss, "What you just said hurt me deeply," that's like telling a rhinoceros he has bad breath. He doesn't care. It doesn't even register.

If you say, "What you're doing is shameful," you're confusing them with a person who is capable of feeling shame. Toxic people immunize themselves against shame with malice, arrogance, and mockery. You can't shame someone who is convinced in their own mind that they are better than you. Your opinion means nothing to them.

Let's go back to the cilantro analogy. Hurting others probably matters to you. Shame is something you want to avoid. But the same activity and charge that you loathe can be something a toxic person loves.

In such instances it's best to just do your job, don't take it personally, limit your contact as much as you can, and do what I usually do—pray for their spouse and kids![1]

Defined by What They Hate

Counselors Dr. Henry Cloud and Dr. John Townsend explain the difference between "proactive" people and "reactive" people, and their description of reactive people comes very close to how we're using the word *toxic*: "Proactive people show you what they love, what they want, what they purpose, and what they stand for. Those people are very different from those who are known by what they hate, what they don't like, what they stand against, and what they will not do."[2]

I'm not calling all reactive people toxic (if you've been hurt or abused, an initial reactive response is an essential stage of healing), but every toxic person I've met seems *mired* in that reactive profile.

---

1. I'm not a trained therapist. The best description for me would be a pastoral counselor—someone who tries to help people understand the Bible and its application to our lives. For more thorough, step-by-step, "how-to" treatment of toxic people from a psychological perspective, consider *Boundaries* by Henry Cloud and John Townsend, *Bold Love* by Dan Allender and Tremper Longman III, and several books by Leslie Vernick (www.leslievernick.com).

They never get out of it. They are known more by what they hate and who they oppose than by who and what they love. Accordingly, they have a negative, toxic, and poisonous effect on you instead of a nurturing, healing, and encouraging effect.

Sometimes those who have a "righteous" cause can be the worst at this. They are so focused on taking others down who may, in fact, be perpetuating an evil that they use evil to fight evil. The Bible urges us not to do that: "Do not repay evil with evil or insult with insult" (1 Peter 3:9).

It's fascinating to meditate on the way Jesus interacted with lepers (I'm not, of course, calling lepers toxic; this is an analogy). People were astonished that Jesus could touch lepers without becoming leprous himself. The miracle wasn't just that the lepers were healed; it was also that Jesus wasn't infected.

Not being "infected" has to be a significant concern when interacting with toxic people. It's not easy to do. One of the most vulnerable times for us to sin is when we are first sinned against. Can we interact with hateful people without becoming hate-filled? Can we stand against abuse without becoming abusive? Can we resist controlling people without trying to control them? Can we confront a murderous spirit without wanting to socially "kill" the murderer? We never feel more justified doing evil than when we are self-righteously confronting evil.

Christians can be particularly beholden to what Francis de Sales described as "rash judgment."[3] We live with a high sense of justice and of what is right and wrong, but that can tempt us as well as instruct us if we don't "baptize" this discernment with grace and empathy. De Sales likens rash judgment to a "spiritual jaundice" that "makes all things appear evil to the eyes of those who are infected with it."[4] He notes that "they who have imbibed pride, envy, ambition, and hatred, think everything they see evil and blameable."[5]

The challenge is that those who have most fallen into pride, envy, ambition, and hatred are the least likely people to see it in themselves. We recognize adultery, drunkenness, and murder, but there's something about these attitudinal sins that blind us spiritually even as they infect us. We think our neighbor smells so bad that we lose the ability to smell our own stink.

This is especially so when, as we just stated, we are sinned against first. That's the threshold through which "rash judgment" quickly passes. If you've been abused by power, you may see the healthy exercise of authority as a "power grab." If you've been sexually harassed, you may be tempted to interpret every compliment as a come-on. If you've awakened to poor teaching in a previous church, you may spend more time in a new church searching for implied heresy than you do opening your heart to conviction. And you'll be *sorely tempted* to respond in all future relationships with "rash judgment" instead of charity. This is not to question the concerns of those who have been victimized but is rather to call all of us to not be prisoners of our own experience as we seek to pursue truth and love in relationships.

We are called as believers to treat others with *charity*. Rash judgment is the opposite of charity. Toxic people deserve to be called out—for what they are doing. We become toxic ourselves, however, when we apply rash judgment to someone not necessarily for what they are doing but for how we are *interpreting* what they are doing in the light of how others sinned against us in the past. We become toxic ourselves when we employ rash judgment, almost with glee, immediately jumping to the conclusion that someone is in the wrong and not going to them personally but rather unleashing a public vendetta to expose them.

Putting It All Together

I chose the cilantro analogy to make an important point. Probably all of us have at times acted with rage, malice, slander, and deception. All of us have tried to control others. A mother whose son is getting into drugs is going to be sorely tempted to control him, but her motivation is concern, not toxicity. All of us have even sought to "murder" in the sense of pulling life out of someone's work or reputation. Individual acts don't make a person toxic; toxic describes someone who feels comfortable in those acts and energized by those acts and who makes those acts the common approach to their relationships.

Biblical counselor Brad Hambrick warns those he counsels, "We don't want to be at our best when we're at our worst." It's a bad sign when conflict makes you more excited than fellowship—when you're energized by taking others on rather than encouraging them.

I sometimes eat cilantro because, especially at Mexican restaurants, they tend to put it in everything, especially the salsa. But I hate it even when I eat it. Sometimes I know I'm eating it, but because I desire what's around it, I put up with it.

In the same way, out of concern, we may try to control a loved one. We may try to get even with someone and gossip. We may slip into seasons of malice. But like a person who has had the flu for five days and starts to feel better, we want to jump into the shower and get the stink off us as soon as possible.

Toxic people enjoy the stink. They stop recognizing it as stink. To them, their smell is delicious. They like it. They love it. They want some more of it.[2]

Toxicity Is a Stew, Not a Soup

Just as an experienced hiker wants to know what poisoned oak, poison ivy, and nettles look like in order to avoid touching them, God's servants need to know toxic people so they can avoid being spiritually assaulted by them. If you're trying to discern whether you're dealing with a truly toxic person or interaction, consider these questions:

- Do your interactions with them require long periods for you to recover?
- Does your relationship with them destroy your peace, joy, strength, and hope?
- Are they interfering with your availability for and participation in other healthy relationships?

---

2. My apologies to Tim McGraw . . .

- Do they exhibit a murderous spirit?
- Are they controlling? Do you feel manipulated by them?
- Do you feel minimized by them?
- Does the person seem to come alive when exhibiting anger, rage, malice, slander, filthy language, and lying?

It's important to point out that not *every* toxic person is controlling. Not *every* toxic person has a murderous spirit. Not *every* toxic person loves hate. Toxicity is a stew with individual elements that can be added or subtracted; it's not a soup where everything is mixed together.

Don't look at these descriptions as boxes to be checked and if two or three are missing, the person is excused from being labeled as toxic. Toxic behavior has many faces and many combinations.

Another thing to remember is that while some people truly are toxic through and through, not everyone is toxic to everyone in the same way. Brad Hambrick points out that "toxicity usually shows up in relationships of high commitment and privacy, like at home or work. If toxicity spreads to more social settings, there is exceedingly high moral decay."[6]

This is helpful for friends and counselors to know because if a spouse or colleague comes to you with stories of someone behaving in a highly toxic way but you've never seen that toxicity displayed, the reason may be that you've never related to them in a context that elicits their toxic behavior. Uninformed pastors hurt a lot of church members when they respond with, "Jim [or Jane] always seems so pleasant every time I talk to them. This can't be true!" Don't add to the victim's misery by initially assuming they're crazy or making things up. Just because you and I haven't seen something ourselves doesn't mean it's never happened.

Some people can become so toxic that kindness dictates we warn others when they are being preyed on. But *humility* calls us to realize that what is toxic for us may not be toxic for others. If you have a toxic experience with someone that leaves you frustrated and discouraged, rethinking conversations late at night, finding your blood pressure rising, and (especially this!) seeing it keep you from being present with loved ones long after the toxic interaction is over, then for you that relationship isn't healthy. But I'm reluctant to too hastily apply the label "toxic" in an absolutist sense.

In one sense, *I'm actually judging myself*. I'm admitting I can't interact with this person in a healthy way. Maybe the problem is with me, or maybe it's with them. Maybe it's with both. But God will have to use someone else to reach them. I can't learn from them, and they can't learn from me, so let's just go our own ways. Most of us aren't professional counselors with the ability to diagnose someone's mental health. A PhD who previewed this book wondered when I would get into diagnoses of mental disorders, but that's beyond my competence, as it is for most of us. There are truly toxic people I would tell my loved ones to simply avoid. If I'm having tremendous difficulty in a relationship and I'm not sure why but it seems like it's toxic, I'm now more inclined to step back without trying to make a diagnosis (which I'm not qualified to make anyway). When we realize the personal effect someone has on us, that's really all we need to know.

You and I both have a unique past, unique personalities, and particular tolerances. There is no one person alive on this planet who can best reach every other individual. That's why God has created a church. Just because I can't reach a person who is toxic for me doesn't mean God doesn't have someone else who can reach that person, someone for whom the person I can't reach isn't toxic. While it would be a waste of time for me to interact with that particular person, God has plenty of servants who can be much more effective and fruitful spending time with them without doing injury to their souls.

As it pertains to you and me, let's admit we can't reach everyone, so let's invest our time in the reliable people we *can* reach. Find out who is toxic *to you*, consider walking away, and entrust them to God.

Takeaways

- Spiritually healthy people love and exhibit compassion, kindness, humility, gentleness, patience, and love. Many toxic people love and exhibit anger, rage, malice, slander, filthy language, and lying.
- It's easier for someone who is on equal footing to confront the toxic behavior of a colleague. Remaining silent perpetuates the victimization of those who don't have the power to speak up for themselves.
- Toxic people often lack empathy and shame; normal appeals in these cases won't work.
- Toxic people often become so focused on what they hate and what they oppose that they lose sight of what they love and are for.
- Following in the footsteps of Jesus, we have to learn how to interact with "lepers" without becoming leprous ourselves. We need to be on our guard against "rash judgment."
- Instead of loving hate, we are invited to love charity.
- Toxic behavior doesn't always come with the same characteristics. A person can be controlling and not murderous. There are different styles of toxicity, which makes toxicity more like a stew than a soup.
- Most of us aren't qualified to professionally diagnose whether someone is toxic or apply other mental health labels. But if our interactions with them feel toxic, that's reason enough to walk away and allow someone else to work with them.

CHAPTER 6

NO TIME TO WASTE

I don't know how much the following episode was dramatized for a Hollywood script, but in the movie *Gettysburg*, General Lee is portrayed as being furious with General J. E. B. Stuart, who took his cavalry and left the Confederate forces all but blind (without sending in reconnaissance reports) during the early days of the famous Civil War battle in Pennsylvania. When Stuart finally returns, Lee chastises him, forcefully informing Stuart that many officers believe Stuart has let all of them down.

Stuart demands to know the officers' names.

Lee responds with conviction: "There is no time for that."

Lee proceeds to scold the cavalry officer for leaving all of them woefully uninformed about the Union's positions and says, to make himself very clear, "This must never happen again."

Stuart flinches at Lee's harsh words, puts down his hat, and pulls out his sword, a sign of resignation. "Since I have lost your confidence . . ."

Lee slams his fist down on a table and screams, "I have told you there is no time for that! *There is no time!*"

Their armies were involved in a furious struggle. Men were literally dying. Which men, and how many, would depend on choices they were making, even as they spoke. There was no time to worry about personal squabbles or hurt egos. All energy had to be focused on the task at hand.

There is no time for that!

This sense of urgency and focus in the midst of physical warfare is not unlike the urgency and focus God's people are called to in the midst of spiritual warfare and our general Christian mission. Jesus,

Paul, Peter, James, John, and even Jude all use the same urgent language to help us understand how vital and pressing our mission before God is:

JESUS: "As long as it is day, we must do the works of him who sent me. Night is coming, when no one can work" (John 9:4).

PAUL: "What I mean, brothers and sisters, is that the time is short . . . This world in its present form is passing away" (1 Corinthians 7:29, 31).

JAMES: "If anyone, then, knows the good they ought to do and doesn't do it, it is sin for them" (James 4:17).

PETER: "You ought to live holy and godly lives as you look forward to the day of God and speed its coming" (2 Peter 3:11–12).

JOHN: "This is how we know what love is: Jesus Christ laid down his life for us. And we ought to lay down our lives for our brothers and sisters . . . Dear children, let us not love with words or speech but with actions and in truth" (1 John 3:16, 18).

JUDE: "I felt compelled to write and urge you to contend for the faith that was once for all entrusted to God's holy people" (Jude 3).

If you are in Christ, you aren't just saved; you are *enlisted*. You have been called into a tremendously important work—an urgent work—and there's no time to lose.

A football player doesn't worry about mowing his lawn the morning of the Super Bowl.

A bride doesn't blow off her wedding to watch a sitcom.

A fireman doesn't finish his sandwich when a building blows up. Why?

They all have more urgent things to do.

That's the attitude we need in the kingdom of God. What *every* believer is doing is crucially important. Because our message is so precious, because the Holy Spirit within us is so powerful, and because the work of building God's kingdom is so necessary, we don't have time to waste.

Jesus told his disciples, "As the Father has sent me, I am sending you" (John 20:21). The classic Christian writer Andrew Murray wrote, "The Lord Jesus gave Himself entirely and undividedly over to accomplish His work; He lived for it alone . . . As with Jesus, so with us. Christ's mission is *the only reason for our being on earth* . . . When I believe this, and like my Lord in His mission consecrate myself undividedly to it, shall I indeed live well-pleasing to Him."[1]

Too many think our salvation is all about us—personal peace, assurance, happiness, and security. One of the greatest needs in the church today is more workers. Not just believers. Not just church attenders. Not even tithers. It is *workers*, those who believe that to be saved isn't to wait for heaven but to get busy bringing heaven's presence and authority to this present earth as ambassadors for Christ.

A More Important Work

In the heart of the Sermon on the Mount, Jesus proclaims the surest path to the fulfilled life, a life without regrets. It is a life based entirely on something outside ourselves: "Seek first his kingdom and his righteousness, and all these things will be given to you as well" (Matthew 6:33–34).

God's kingdom is his rule, his reign, the extension of his presence into all crevices of life and society. He is empowering believers with his Holy Spirit to be participants in this process as they proclaim and work for God's justice, mercy, and truth. The force of the Greek language speaks of a *continuous* task: "*keep on seeking* the kingdom of God." No Christian ever retires from this work. To be a Christian is to keep seeking, above all else, the kingdom of God.

What does this mean practically? It means when you and I wake up, God's agenda is more important to us than our agendas, and we dare not stop praying until that is so. We weren't saved to feel safe or simply be freed from worry about our eternal destiny. Those things are true and precious, but in the here and now, we are saved to embrace this kingdom work: Christ "died for all, that those who live should live no longer for themselves, but for him who died for them and was raised again" (2 Corinthians 5:15).

Christ died for me and you *so that* we start living for him instead of for ourselves. You and I don't own our time, our talents, or our treasure. We are to expend all that we are and all that we have to participate in the building of God's kingdom. Whatever office God has placed you in, whatever household, whatever community; whether you are healthy or ill; wealthy or just barely making it; lonely or socially overbooked, life is richest when you give each moment of each day to God with the prayer, "Let me receive your love and pour it out on these people so that I can represent you every minute of the day."

The early church wasn't defined by its sermons and songs; it was magnified by its mission, embraced by every member.

Fruitful

Many of us grew up with a "negative" faith: Don't do this or that; don't say this or that; don't visit that place or think that thought. In other words, we don't want to create sin. But if our focus is on consistently *not* doing something, at the end of our life all we'll have done is . . . *nothing*. We'll have been like dead people walking with nothing to show for our time on earth.

A corpse doesn't "sin." But does a corpse display the glory of God? Jesus defines *fruitfulness* as being a necessary part of *faithfulness*:

Then [Jesus] told this parable: "A man had a fig tree growing in his vineyard, and he went to look for fruit on it but did not find any. So he said to the man who took care of the vineyard, 'For three years now I've been coming to look for fruit on this fig tree and haven't found any. Cut it down! Why should it use up the soil?'

"'Sir,' the man replied, 'leave it alone for one more year, and I'll dig around it and fertilize it. If it bears fruit next year, fine! If not, then cut it down.'"

LUKE 13:6–8

You may be asking, "What does all this have to do with toxic people?"

Everything.

This is the chapter I couldn't wait to get to. I wish I could have made it the first chapter, but my editor wisely told me to wait until now. This book puts dealing with toxic people into a spiritual, not psychological, perspective. It's not about protecting yourself from toxic people (though that's a valid aim); it's more about protecting your mission from toxic attacks.

If life is about accomplishing a very particular task, then "obedience" and the "right thing to do" must mean accomplishing that one particular task—seeking first God's kingdom, bearing fruit in his name, and, in the words of Titus 3:14, being devoted "to doing what is good."

If I send an employee to a gas station to fill the gas tank of a company car and they return to the office saying, "I had a great conversation with Skip. I washed the windshield. I picked up some litter in the parking lot. And I even brought back donuts for the entire office" but he didn't fill the gas tank, has he really been obedient? He may have done some good and noble things, but those other things got in the way of the first thing.

Worse, if he added, "And you should be proud of me because I didn't steal from anyone, run over anyone, gossip about anyone, or lie to anyone."

Fine, *but did you fill the gas tank*? That's why you were sent out.

The call to seek *first* the kingdom of God is the foundation for how we can biblically respond to toxic people. If you're not a Christian, this book is likely to disappoint you, as it is focused on helping God's people accomplish God's work in God's way. From this perspective, learning how to deal with toxic people isn't first and foremost about protecting our joy, our peace, our reputation, or even our sanity (though these are good aims). It's primarily about protecting our *mission*. We are saved to be fruitful. We are enlisted in a great and holy work. We don't have time to be distracted by clever people who soak up all our energy and efforts in a hopeless cause. Pouring ourselves out on toxic people is spiritually like trying to wash rain. It's a waste of time that keeps us from more fruitful endeavors.

And your kingdom work *does matter.* You need to know this, feel this, live this, to be rightfully protected from toxic attacks. You may not be widely recognized as God's worker, but just as wars are won through the secret sacrifices of unknown soldiers, so God's kingdom is built on the backs of faithful and quiet servants.

When my son worked with Boston Consulting Group, though only a young man in his mid-twenties, he was working on a daily basis with the executive leadership of two major companies that were merging. When he was visiting us at home, my wife needed us to buy something from one of the stores involved in the potential merger. As Graham and I walked into the store, I thought to myself, *Neither the store manager nor certainly any of the clerks have any idea how much influence my son may be having on their future employment.* The decisions he was a part of would soon have a direct impact on their daily lives, but he was working behind the scenes and looked way too young to carry that much clout.

But he did.

I thought of that scenario when I was asked to speak to a number of military couples from Fort Bragg, most of whom served in special ops. It was a bit unnerving when I realized any one of these soldiers could literally kill me with their bare hands inside of ten seconds if they wanted to. And the chaplain told me right before the conference began, "You shouldn't think everyone in here is a believer. They're not, but they all know you are, so we thought we'd try it out and see how it goes."

If I were to see any of these soldiers shopping in a grocery store, particularly if they were wearing civilian clothes, I wouldn't have any idea how much I owe them. What they're willing to do and what their families are willing to endure and risk so we can enjoy freedom is beyond what I can imagine. Because much of what they do can't and won't be publicized, they will never be fully thanked (certainly not sufficiently by the size of their paycheck). But their mission is essential to the future of our government, and therefore to the future of our national well-being.

God's kingdom servants are like my son and the special ops members: they (you) wield way more influence and power and authority than anyone else may recognize on this side of eternity.

When you're "just an aide," not an elected official, but you play a key role in stopping a piece of disastrous legislation or inspire the passing of a wise one . . .

When you take a chance on a young man or woman who really needs a job . . .

When you faithfully raise a family to love, honor, and serve God . . .

When you walk through someone else's long-term sickness . . .

When you help hold someone accountable for destructive behavior, while also patiently teaching them to apply grace and inviting them into community in order to push back the shame and self-loathing that fuels so much bad behavior . . .

When you share your faith and your reason for believing with someone who will never be famous and may never tell anyone else about it . . .

. . . *you are advancing God's kingdom. You are adding to heaven's glory. You are writing the stories that will be told in eternity.*

Only God knows how crucial our "invisible" work may be, but since Jesus makes it clear that "the last will be first, and the first will be last" (Matthew 20:16), we can expect some major surprises when we compare who is actually celebrated most in life after life.

Active Opposition

This world may not *reward* your mission before God; it will more likely *oppose* it. Virtually every good work is eventually besieged by toxic attacks. The more important the work, the more you can expect attacks. Thus, to complete your work, you have to learn how to recognize, disarm, or step aside from such attacks. In other words, you have to learn how to play defense.

Abraham Lincoln lived with a compelling sense of urgency as he faced vicious personal attacks, one right after the other. Lincoln's personal writings make clear that he believed his destiny before God was to preserve the relatively new experiment called democracy. At the time the United States declared its independence, no other true democracy existed. The United States was trying something new, and it wasn't easy.[1] Lincoln believed preserving the world's largest democratic nation intact was worth fighting for, and the cost of that conflict (hundreds of thousands of men fell) was such that he was maligned, ridiculed, challenged, and all but ordered to stop. Here's how he responded: "If I were to try to read, much less answer, all the attacks made on me, this shop might as well be closed for any other business. I do the very best I know how—the very best I can; and I mean to keep doing so until the end."[2]

Today, 123 out of 192 countries claim to be democracies (whether they actually *are*, of course, is a matter of fair debate). Abraham Lincoln was treated viciously by toxic people, but the legacy he left behind, the work he accomplished, his ability to show that holding a democracy together is possible even when citizens violently disagree with each other, has dramatically shaped world history.

Your mission may not be as visible. It likely won't be celebrated (or challenged) in history books. But in God's eyes, it is no less urgent and valuable: "Therefore, my dear brothers and sisters, stand firm. Let nothing move you. Always give yourselves fully to the work of the Lord, because you know that your labor in the Lord is not in vain" (1 Corinthians 15:58).

Toxic People Attack

As did Abraham Lincoln, you will soon learn that any God-given mission attracts opposition, and that's where toxic people come into play. This was a lesson I had to learn when I first entered a bit of public

---

1. I fully realize that the United States is more accurately described as a republic, not a true democracy, but our system of government is based on the best principles of democracy while trying to safeguard against the worst tendencies of a democracy.

ministry, as I was initially surprised by the intensity of the personal attacks. I don't want to intentionally hurt anyone. I mean that. I try, before God and by his grace, to live by Romans 13:10, which teaches that "love does *no* harm to a neighbor" (emphasis added). In fact, I don't remember the last time I intentionally harmed someone, verbally or otherwise.

Knowing my intentions before God, it was a bit of a shock when people started attacking me. I have a pretty conservative approach to Scripture. I tend to think the clearest meaning, especially one the church has had throughout almost its entire history, is the one we should accept and aspire to, which I understand can be considered "mean" if Scripture appears to question something someone wants to do.

Added to this, however, was the sometimes seemingly deliberate misrepresentation. I have had to come to grips with the fact that people have lied and will lie about me; they will rip a few sentences out of context, twist a few passages, and make me sound like I believe something I don't because they need something to be angry about and oppose. And they'll post it all on an Amazon review or in a blog.

It has taken me too long to learn that it's often best to simply not respond.[2] Here's what I've come to terms with in regard to mission: My first goal in life isn't to defend *me*. What someone thinks about me won't impact their future spiritual destiny. For every minute someone lies about me, I want to spend an hour telling others the truth about Jesus Christ. I don't want to be distracted even to defend myself.

Why?

God's kingdom is more important than mine. Infinitely more important. *There's no time* for lesser concerns. Jesus urged his disciples, "As long as it is day, we must do the works of him who sent me" (John 9:4).

Without this sense of mission, I could waste a lot of time and energy (something I've done at times in the past). Understanding the

---

2. One could make an exception, of course, if a spouse needs to defend her or his reputation during a custody dispute, or something similar.

brilliance and depth of Matthew 6:33—seeking first the kingdom of God, not my kingdom, reputation, or comfort—keeps me on course to live a life that matters most.

I hope this book will deliver you from engaging in "fantasy arguments" with toxic people in your head or "Facebook fights" online. Armed with an acute sense of mission, you will realize that sometimes (though not always) defending your reputation is a waste of time when you could be focusing your energy on proclaiming the glory of God.

A Final Warning

The reason this book is anchored in talking about mission is deliberate and crucial. Otherwise, this book could be misunderstood and used for destructive aims. Our mission is *not* to seek out and defeat toxic people. In most instances, unless we have vocational authority over them, our job is to ignore them so we don't get distracted from our mission to love others. The *mission* is our focus; toxic people are merely the *distraction* we need to avoid.

Celebrated novelist and philosopher Aldous Huxley warns, "Those who crusade not *for* God in themselves, but *against* the devil in others, never succeed in making the world better, but leave it either as it was, or sometimes even perceptibly worse than it was before the crusade began. By thinking primarily of evil we tend, however excellent our intentions, to create occasions for evil to manifest itself . . . To be more *against* the devil than *for* God is exceedingly dangerous. Every crusader is apt to go mad. He is haunted by the wickedness which he attributes to his enemies; it becomes in some sort a part of him."[3]

Christians are called to love generously and even sacrificially, and that includes loving some very difficult people. If you think your job is to spot and confront toxic people for the sake of stopping toxic people, you'll miss the entire point of this book. An earlier subtitle for this book (later swapped for the current one) was "choosing service to God over submission to toxic people." Service comes first;

everything else flows from that. If I'm driving down the highway eager to get somewhere, I'm not going to stop whenever I see litter on the roadside. However, if something is blocking the road, I have to stop the car, jump out, and move it out of the way to get to where I'm going.

That should be your attitude with toxic people. Leave them in the hands of God when you can. Confront and remove them when you must. But always keep your focus on seeking first the kingdom of God.

Takeaways

- Jesus and his early followers speak of a necessary *urgency* in carrying out God's work.
- One of the church's greatest needs today is more workers who embrace Jesus' call to keep seeking first the kingdom of God.
- Seeking first God's kingdom means his agenda becomes more important than our own; we offer all we have and are to his service, regardless of our vocation or station in life.
- Jesus defines fruitfulness as a necessary part of faithfulness. More than focusing on avoiding sin, we are called to eagerly embrace good deeds.
- Learning how to handle toxic people, for the purposes of this book, is more about preserving our mission than it is about defending ourselves.
- Those who have the "quietest" ministry on earth may be celebrated most loudly in heaven.
- We will be attacked as we serve God, but we need to avoid getting distracted. In most cases, our job isn't to defend ourselves; it's to focus on fulfilling God's agenda.
- We don't need to search out toxic people; they'll reveal themselves. Build your life on the positive work of seeking first God's kingdom, not on the negative work of exposing and tearing down toxic people.

CHAPTER 7

RELIABLE PEOPLE

My wife and I will be forever grateful to a wonderful campus ministry at Western Washington University in Bellingham, Washington, named Campus Christian Fellowship. Our campus pastor, Brady Bobbink, didn't let any student graduate without knowing 2 Timothy 2:2 by heart: "And the things you have heard me say in the presence of many witnesses entrust to reliable people who will also be qualified to teach others."

We talked often about "2 Timothy 2:2ing" the world. Brady focused our ministry on evangelism and discipleship with an intentional focus on finding reliable people, qualified to teach others, in whom we could invest our lives.

At eighteen years of age, I wasn't sure I had that much to invest in others, but Brady used kingdom theology to make the mission sound compelling: Don't worry about what you don't yet have. Just give whatever God has given you.

I've never stopped looking for those reliable people.

Shortly after I arrived in Houston in 2010, I got a message from a high school student who was writing an apologetic for the Christian faith. It was a pretty ambitious effort, but this kid was actually pulling it off. That young man and I walked through the rest of his high school years, his college years, further studies in England, and his eventual return to Houston, where he is launching a business.

Lisa knows that when his name comes up on my phone, unless what I'm doing is particularly urgent, I answer it. I'm committed to that young man because I believe he is reliable and qualified to teach others.

A married couple invited Lisa and me to lunch in the middle of a destination marriage conference I was speaking at. They live in Dallas, and the husband, Mark, travels to Houston once or twice a month for business. He asked me if I would consider mentoring him when he's in town, but with everything I had going on at Second Baptist and my outside writing and speaking, I couldn't say yes. But I agreed to meet with him for runs once a month. I didn't know much about him, and a mentoring relationship is a serious thing that I wasn't yet willing to commit to.

As we ran, he shared his vision for encouraging men in a particular area. We talked informally about what he needed to set up before launching his ministry. And then about two years later, he mentioned the advice he had received from a former Navy Seal that he needed to set up a "diamond formation" before going into battle.

By that time, I was willing to be part of his "diamond formation." This is a reliable man I believe God can and will use. It's a worthy investment. We met for a couple years as friends, and I still consider him a friend first, but now, having seen his reliability, I'm willing to do the spiritual work of also being a part of his ministry oversight.

Jesus chose his disciples, and we should choose ours. As a pastor, I spend plenty of time with people who are hurting and need help working through a particular issue or understanding how to apply a sermon or Scripture. But if I'm devoting extended time and thought to someone outside a normal friendship, it's because I believe we're in a 2 Timothy 2:2 situation.

We should be looking for people to invest in. If I'm already living a full schedule because there are reliable people and kingdom-minded work filling up my calendar, it is much easier to say no to someone who just wants to take up time and be noticed in a toxic sort of way. If our schedule is already full doing good things, we won't feel so guilty about saying no to less productive encounters.

This priority to put our first and best efforts into reliable people is a biblical call, not a personal preference. Of course, as God's followers we are always open, twenty-four hours a day, to divine appointments to love. The good Samaritan didn't check whether the beaten-up traveler was reliable. *We want to be generous to all, but focused on a few,* as Jesus was. He healed and served and then often sent the recipients home.

Before you wrestle with how to handle toxic people, let me ask how many reliable people you're investing in. I'm not trying to get anyone out of difficult relationships; my first focus is to get people into healthy discipleship relationships. The reason I've learned to avoid toxic people and limit my exposure to them is not because I don't want to be bothered. As a Christian, I live to be "bothered" in the sense that I'm called to love God in part by *loving others*. My time isn't my own! Other people's needs come before mine.

No. I limit my exposure to toxic people because I'm devoted to growing God's church, and doing that requires me to be on the lookout for reliable people who are qualified to teach others, and then to respond by being generous with my time as I invest in their spiritual welfare.

Can I make this personal? One of my daughters has been in several churches as she moves around the country. One of the most painful things for her has been that male pastors (like me) often recruit younger men, while younger professional women can be treated as if they don't even exist (or are simply asked to volunteer in the nursery). If you are an older woman (even if you're only in your thirties, you're older than a woman in her twenties), it would mean so very much if you'd take another woman under your wings and invest in her.

If you have a particular profession, find other young women who would value the opportunity to spend time with a woman in their field. If you're in academia, if you got married rather young and are raising kids without outside employment, if you are single and "kicking it" in the business world, find younger women on a similar path and reach out to them.

It's not like they have to be on the same vocational path as you, however. Several guys I work with aren't going into the ministry. But they love God. They want to know how to pray. They want more of God's understanding. I'm not suggesting we have to invest only in people who are doing (or planning to do) exactly what we do—but find someone on a similar journey toward God and reach out to them. Make yourself available.

The approach we're talking about here isn't about working *less*; it's about working more *efficiently* and more *strategically*.

John Climacus, who in the seventh century wrote what became the most widely used handbook of monastic living in the Eastern church, puts together beautifully what we've been saying: "In any conflict with unbelievers or heretics, we should stop after we have twice reproved them (cf. Titus 3:10). But where we are dealing with those who are eager to learn the truth, we should never grow tired of doing the right thing (cf. Gal. 6:9). And we should use both situations to test our own steadfastness."[1]

We have to learn how to say no to the toxic people so we can give a hearty yes to the reliable people.

Jesus' Reliable People

Paul put words to the practice of 2 Timothy 2:2ing the world, but Jesus laid down the example. Jesus let the rich young ruler walk away from him and instead of chasing after him, he turned to the reliable people, the disciples, to explain what had just happened.

An even starker example occurs during the Last Supper. Before Judas left to betray Jesus, our Lord could have said the word and his eleven faithful disciples would have pinned Judas to the ground and kept him from leaving. Instead, Jesus all but sends Judas away: "What you are about to do, do quickly" (John 13:27).

Notice what happens next. As soon as Judas is gone, Jesus unleashes some of the most precious and powerful words in all of Scripture. He talks about the Son of Man being glorified, tells them he is going away (so they'll be able to figure out what happened after the fact), and then launches into that beautiful passage on love: "A new command I give you: Love one another. As I have loved you, so you must love one another. By this everyone will know that you are my disciples, if you love one another" (John 13:34–35).

He then comforts his disciples because he knows they are soon going to be overwhelmed with grief, assuring them that though they will not be able to immediately follow, they eventually will follow. He tells them not to let their hearts be troubled, gives them revelatory insights about him being "the way and the truth and the life" (John 14:6), tells them in no uncertain terms that he's not just a prophet but he's God incarnate ("anyone who has seen me has seen the Father," John 14:9) and then talks about sending the Holy Spirit, following that up with the secret to being fruitful (the vine and the branches), *and so much more.*

Dismissing the one toxic person was like opening up the floodgates to some of the most powerful time of teaching this world has ever seen. These chapters rival the Sermon on the Mount in their power, majesty, and truth.

Jesus lets the one toxic person go do his toxic work, turns to his reliable men, and fills them up with truth. It almost reads as if he couldn't wait to let the toxic person go so he could invest so heavily and powerfully into the minds and hearts of the reliable people who remained.

Reliable Resistance

Rosaria Butterfield taught English and women's studies at Syracuse University in the 1990s. Her primary academic field was critical theory, and she specialized in queer theory. Rosaria also advised the LGBT student group, wrote Syracuse University's policy for same-sex couples, and actively lobbied for LGBT aims alongside her lesbian partner.[2]

She started researching the Religious Right in 1997 and "their politics of hatred against people like me." After she wrote an article attacking the Promise Keepers—a ministry focused on building up men—she got a response from Ken Smith, a local pastor. Ken didn't argue or attack Rosaria for her article; he just asked her "to explore and defend the presuppositions that undergirded it."[3]

Out of curiosity and for research purposes as much as anything, Rosaria accepted Ken's invitation for dinner at their house, "conscious of my butch haircut and the gay and pro-choice bumper stickers on my car."[4] Ken and his wife's hospitality (they didn't turn the air-conditioning on and served a vegetarian dinner—two issues that mattered greatly to Rosaria) became a threshold through which Rosaria could go to begin her two-year walk to Jesus.

Ken's humble prayer before dinner disarmed Rosaria, but after the prayer, her defenses immediately went up again. "I remember holding my breath and waiting to be punched in the stomach with something grossly offensive. I believed at this time that God was dead and that if he ever was alive, the fact of poverty, violence, racism, sexism, homophobia, and war was proof that he didn't care about his creation. I believed that religion was, as Marx wrote, the opiate of the masses, an imperialist social construction made to soothe the existential angst of the intellectually impaired. But Ken's God seemed alive, three-dimensional, and wise, if firm. And Ken and Floy were anything but intellectually impaired."[5]

The Smiths kept engaging Rosaria with meals and private conversations, including many at Rosaria's house, and waited two years before actually inviting her to church. Rosaria says that if they had rushed the church invitation, "I would have careened like a skateboard off a cliff, and would have never come back."[6]

The Smiths' gracious hospitality forms the basis for Rosaria's third book, *The Gospel Comes with a House Key: Practicing Radically Ordinary Hospitality in Our Post-Christian World*.[7] Not only did Rosaria become a believer, but she has become a unique voice in the Christian community as a writer, speaker, and guest on various programs.

Her story is a stark reminder that initial resistance isn't necessarily "toxic."

Notice that Jesus didn't always walk away at the first sign of resistance. He figured out *why* a person was resisting and responded accordingly. If the reason wasn't toxic, Jesus often walked *toward* someone rather than away.

For example, after Jesus performed a miracle with fish, Simon Peter "fell at Jesus' knees and said, "Go away from me, Lord; I am a sinful man!" (Luke 5:8).

Peter's resistance was based in fear and shame. Far from walking away, Jesus moved toward this reliable man, qualified to teach others, saying, "'Don't be afraid; from now on you will fish for people.' So they pulled their boats up on shore, left everything and followed him" (Luke 5:10–11).

Notice *they* pulled their boats up and followed Jesus. Following Peter's example, James and John also "left everything and followed him." By reaching Peter, Jesus reached many others.

Given her background, Rosaria Butterfield has had a particular entrée into the lives of many others who might see the church as a threat instead of as a beacon of hope. Ken's wise and patient approach proved to be a tremendously valuable kingdom investment. How sad it would be if we thought someone's initial resistance meant they weren't "reliable" or "qualified to teach others."

How did Ken know Rosaria wasn't toxic and was a worthy investment? People might expect that initial conversations between Ken and Rosaria were heated, but both deny that that was so. Ken points out that "Rosaria and I could both distinguish between acceptance and approval." Rosaria certainly attacked "Moral Majority" types, but Ken didn't take that personally, instead responding, "Yes, but who is *Jesus*?"

Rosaria remembers, "Ken never really took my bait, and I'm not a debater . . . We always had really good conversations."[8]

What distinguished Rosaria in that moment from the toxic resisters we've been talking about was an openness to engage. Ken freely admits that his real aim in approaching Rosaria was getting an entrée to her students. He wanted an opportunity to let young men and women at Syracuse hear a reasoned defense of the Christian faith. Rosaria wouldn't allow *that*. Instead, she asked Ken if he would take on a "student of one" and give her a full-out explanation of why "this one book [the Bible] is true."

If someone gives you a door that wide-open, don't walk; *run* toward them! By reaching Rosaria, Ken has reached hundreds of thousands who have been touched by her faith, wisdom, and insight.

If you are working with someone who seems to disagree with

everything you believe to be true but they want to hear why you believe what you believe—and the conversations are productive (which means you have to listen and seek to understand their position as well)—you're doing exactly what 2 Timothy 2:2 and Matthew 6:33 call you to do. *Disagreement isn't toxic.* Toxicity speaks to a person's state of heart and mind. Rosaria was a bit hostile, to be sure, but hostility alone doesn't rise to the level of a controlling, murderous personality that loves hate, won't listen, and only wants to bring you down.

If we want to truly walk in the footsteps of Jesus, all of us will be willing to walk *away* from toxic encounters so we can walk *toward* reliable people.

Takeaways

- The obedient Christian life is a life of finding reliable people in whom we can invest all that God has given to us.
- Learning to play defense and disengage from toxic people isn't about saving time for our own pleasure. Rather, it's about working more efficiently and strategically as we seek first the kingdom of God.
- Jesus models the practice of letting a toxic person walk away and then investing his time teaching reliable people (instead of running after the toxic one).
- Ken and Rosaria's friendship teaches us that resistance and disagreement shouldn't be equated with toxicity. As long as the relationship is productive and non-debilitating, that's what ministry is all about.
- Jesus discerned *why* a person was resisting before he chose to walk away.

CHAPTER 8

PIGS AND PEARLS

Whenever I preach on gentleness, I know I'll raise the ire of at least one earnest person who will fidget through the sermon, bursting to jump out of their chair as soon as the service is over to ask me, "But what about when Jesus overturned the money changers' tables in the temple?"

The Bible is quite explicit about the fact that Jesus was marked by gentleness. The Old Testament prophesied that the Messiah would be gentle (Zechariah 9:9; Matthew 21:5). Jesus used only two virtues to describe himself, one of which is gentle (Matthew 11:29). And when the early church—those who had witnessed Jesus' life and ministry firsthand—remembered Jesus, they remembered his gentleness (2 Corinthians 10:1). Given that it was predicted Jesus would be gentle, Jesus described himself as gentle, and the early church remembered him as gentle, I believe you can preach a pretty compelling sermon that we should pursue gentleness as well.

But what about that money changers' scene?

The clearing of the temple is actually the scene that all but *confirms* Jesus' gentleness in this sense: the reason this incident struck a nerve is that it seemed so unlike Jesus' normal mode of operating. When a mom or dad yells all the time, a kid learns to tune that parent out. When a normally placid parent raises his or her voice, ears perk up. Notice, this is one of the few acts of Jesus recorded in *all four gospels*.[1] There was something that made it particularly memorable to anyone who wanted to tell Jesus' story.

---

1. Matthew 21:12–13; Mark 11:15–17; Luke 19:45–46; John 2:13–22.

Virtues like gentleness aren't always absolutes. Proverbs 26:4–5 contains perhaps the most famous example of this:

> Do not answer a fool according to his folly,
>   or you yourself will be just like him.
> Answer a fool according to his folly,
>   or he will be wise in his own eyes.

Which is it?

The application of wisdom is sort of like defensive driving. Sometimes you need to use the brakes to avoid an accident; sometimes (far less often) it's best to step on the gas pedal, speed up, and move around the danger. Jesus was most often gentle, which forceful people are reluctant to admit. Jesus was sometimes strategically confrontational, which timid people tend to ignore.

Jesus walked away from many toxic people who wanted to hurt him. He didn't walk away from the cross.

The fact is, we usually make a virtue out of our *disposition* rather than our *duty*. If you only have one play—gentleness—it's going to become a problem when the other team's offense demands that you employ a different strategy. When handling toxic people, you don't always enjoy the luxury of doing what comes naturally to you.

If you're like me, preferring to be gentle most of the time, this may be a painful chapter for you. I'd much prefer to write a book about how we should love everyone extravagantly, sacrificially, and enthusiastically. And I'll admit, there should be a hundred books on loving people like that for every one book like this. But this kind of book isn't written very often, which allows toxic people to prey on unsuspecting believers from the shadows.

Jesus was careful not to let that happen. In his own words, he exposes toxic people and what they are doing. If you think it is always wrong to write someone off, even temporarily, even if they are destroying you and your family, what are you going to do with the fact that Jesus explicitly warns us about playing defense against "dogs" and "pigs"?

Dogs

One of Jesus' most notorious sayings (in the minds of some) concerns the kind of people we are labeling as toxic. And Jesus warns us we better learn to play some defense when coming across such people: "Do not give dogs what is sacred; do not throw your pearls to pigs. If you do, they may trample them under their feet, and turn and tear you to pieces" (Matthew 7:6).

When Jesus tells his disciples not to give what is holy to dogs, he's *not* referring to Fifi or Spot, the family pet. Egyptians favored dogs and owned some impressive ones, but Jesus was talking to Jews, who most definitely did *not* keep dogs as pets. Dogs in Jewish quarters were unclean mongrels that scoured the city dumps. They were mean, wild, stinky, filthy animals. Forget Lassie; think of a wild, predatory mongrel with bad breath, yellow teeth, and open sores.

Jesus said there are people just like that, and we shouldn't give those people what is holy because they can't appreciate it.

There's a stark contrast between the vileness of the dogs and the sanctity of the food. This isn't just wholesome, organic food. It is kosher, consecrated food. Such food is not easy to find, prepare, or store, so a Jew would never give kosher food to a mongrel. These mutts ate disgusting stuff all the time—why waste kosher on them?

My wife *did* feed our Golden Retriever, Amber (perhaps the sweetest dog that's ever lived), "sacred" food. We frequented a special pet store that sells human-grade, organic dog food. I didn't question the cost because Lisa said, "Amber's health is important to me!"

That's why I couldn't help laughing when we were on a family walk and Amber took off running. When we caught up to her, she was scarfing down a discarded hot dog along the trail.

Lisa yelled at her, "*I feed you human-grade, grain-free food, and you're eating a HOT DOG on a white bun?*"

Amber may have been a sweet pet, but she was also, when you get down to it, an ignorant beast. She didn't understand the need to control her diet. To her, a hot dog with a bazillion preservatives on a white bun was as heavenly as human-grade, organic, grain-free dog food.

Jesus is telling his followers that some people spiritually are no more discerning than Amber was physically when it came to food. You can give them the best, but they won't appreciate it. It will be wasted on them. They will reject the very best, the purest, and the most compelling truth, *so don't waste your time on them*. Learn to play a little defense.

A Pig and Pearls

When Jesus talked about pearls, most of us today probably think of a string of pearls. In Jesus' day, a string of pearls was exceedingly rare. Pearls were way beyond the budget of all but the wealthiest, and a *string* of pearls would be reserved for royalty. Pearls were difficult to find, and synthetic pearls hadn't been invented yet. That explains why Jesus talked about a man who sold all he had for a *single* pearl. They were so valuable that even one could be worth everything else you own.

But what happens when you throw something that valuable to a pig? The beast tries to eat it. The hard pearl won't break down when he chews it, however, so he will spit it out and charge you in anger. He thinks you're teasing him. He'd rather have pig slop—which you could buy a lifetime's supply of for that one pearl he just spit out—than the treasure you gave him.

A pig is utterly incapable of appreciating the value of a pearl.

That doesn't mean the pearl isn't valuable; it just means the pig is stupid. And you're wasting your time giving a valuable gift to a toxic person.

I know this sounds harsh, but hang with me, because I've found this one sentence spoken by Jesus to be a pretty effective Rorschach test. If you live with a high sense of mission (based on Matthew 6:33 and 2 Timothy 2:2), this sentence is gold; it's such godly, helpful wisdom, and it makes perfect sense.

If you live for yourself, Jesus' sentence sounds mean, cruel, and insensitive.

Here's why it's wise: Jesus is essentially saying that a spiritually dead person is as insensitive to the glory of God's truth as a pig is to the value of a pearl. Because they live by baser instincts, they can't even recognize the value of God's truth. They want something baser. They live on a more primitive level spiritually. They think to themselves, *What good is the gospel? I can't drink it. I can't smoke it. I can't have sex with it. I can't spend it. It doesn't make me laugh, and I can't make myself the center of it. Ppppffffggg!*

That sounds unkind if it's stated as a judgment. But Jesus is telling his followers they have to make such an evaluation not to feel superior (that would be a sin) or to look down on them (which would also be a sin), but to know whether their time is being well-spent and well-invested *because their mission is so urgent*.

Since Jesus ends the gospel of Matthew with a call to preach far and wide, we can discern that he isn't saying we shouldn't share the gospel with nonbelievers, but rather that we *should be prepared to walk away* from the anti-Christ zealots who violently hate God and are in active opposition against him. If they are in a toxic state, even the best, clearest truth won't save them.

When people's eternal destiny is at stake, we don't have time for sentimental niceties. Jesus seems to be saying that it's entirely possible to become so anti-God, so closed to the truth, so rebellious in your heart and mind, that you become a spiritual "dog" or a spiritual "pig." As the apostle Paul writes, "Those who are unspiritual do not receive the gifts of God's Spirit, for they are foolishness to them, and they are unable to understand them because they are spiritually discerned" (1 Corinthians 2:14 NRSV).

When this is the condition of a person's heart, only a direct act of God can melt such a soul—not you. Your best argument won't work. Being nice to them and serving them won't work. Apologizing for every Christian who has ever sinned against them won't work. Distinguishing yourself from every pastor who has ever said anything that offended them won't work. Why? They have a toxic heart that wants to attack and hurt, not a mind that wants to learn. If you engage them, they won't change, *but you'll be attacked*. Jesus wants you to play defense in such situations.

In essence, Jesus is working from Proverbs 9:7–8, which warns, "Whoever corrects a mocker invites insults; whoever rebukes the wicked incurs abuse. Do not rebuke mockers or they will hate you; rebuke the wise and they will love you." This is Proverbs' way of saying, "Don't waste your time on pigs or dogs; instead, find reliable, wise people and invest in them."

It's Not the Fruit's Fault

You can take the most fertile seed known to humankind, pour it out on I-10 all the way from Florida to California, and nothing is going to happen. It's not that there's something wrong with the seed; there's something wrong with the surface that won't receive it.

If we're not careful, we can inadvertently, albeit with good intentions, cheapen the gospel by appearing desperate, as if our own faith will be validated only if the person we are talking to eventually agrees with us. Someone's agreement with Jesus' message of faith doesn't make it more true, and their rejection doesn't make it less true. It is true on its own. The one hearing the word is the one being tested. The word itself is never under judgment. Our faith isn't validated when we can persuade others to agree with us; our faith is validated because it's true. Our faith is validated by the resurrection.

Evangelism is not simply about intellectual persuasion; it requires the supernatural conviction of the Holy Spirit to be effective. If that's not present, we're wasting our time. Evangelism is a work *with* God far more than it is a work *for* God.

Another way of looking at this is to see outreach ministry as "spiritual triage." Just like a battlefield surgeon sometimes has to make the horrific call that a soldier is too far gone to save and therefore he has to leave him because there are so many others who still might be saved if he can only get to them in time, so we have to realize that spending time trying to save someone who isn't ready to be saved means losing others who are.

Perhaps this is why Jesus pleads with his church to pray for more workers (Luke 10:2). Jesus realizes that at the present time (humanly speaking), we have limited resources, so we must use what we do have for the greatest effect.

Some of you may understandably object, "But if we cut off people like this, who will be saved?"

Here's how I've learned to handle this dilemma. Four words have helped me focus and conserve so much time: *No conviction? No counsel.*

We have to learn to discern whether God is already working in this person's heart. We don't chase after people. We should be patient and generous with true, earnest seekers. But if someone seems hard-set against what we're saying, we don't take it personally and we don't argue. That just makes them despise us anyway, which in turn tends to make them despise our message. There's a big difference between reasoning and arguing, by the way. In the end, we're asking ourselves in the back of our minds, *Is there conviction here?*

It may be that God's plan for this person is for you to say one sentence, listen to the objection, and then walk away, waiting for someone else to pick it up—perhaps someone better suited to reach this kind of person (again, just because you can't persuade them doesn't mean someone else isn't better suited to do so).

Sharing God's love and truth is a *spiritual* exercise as much as it is an intellectual one. Remember that Jesus said, "Light has come into the world, but people loved darkness instead of light because their deeds were evil. Everyone who does evil hates the light, and will not come into the light for fear that their deeds will be exposed" (John 3:19–20).

If you're working with a toxic, hard-hearted person, you're dealing with someone who, absent a supernatural touch from God, will hate any light that you shine, no matter how gently, patiently, and gracefully you share it. They don't want their evil to be challenged or exposed. The problem isn't with the light—the light is perfect, holy, and good. The problem is that they hate the light. You can't change that.

So you wait while giving yourself freely and generously to reliable people. You don't necessarily write the toxic person off, of course (though in some cases, you may). As God leads, you can pray that

God will bring conviction or that the sin and destructiveness they're choosing will so disappoint them that they'll finally become open to wisdom and truth. Love them generously, as long as that attention isn't taking you down and keeping you from your calling.

Just because your words can't reach them doesn't at all mean they are beyond reach. God is still working on them, often through what Henry Cloud and John Townsend call "the law of sowing and reaping."[1] God has so set up this world that sin and toxicity have their own consequences: "A man reaps what he sows. Whoever sows to please their flesh, from the flesh will reap destruction; whoever sows to please the Spirit, from the Spirit will reap eternal life" (Galatians 6:7–8). A life of continued toxicity becomes its own punishment. *Let the natural consequences of toxic behavior do their work in opening up a toxic person's heart.* If you try to bring the cure before the patient knows she needs a cure, you'll create resentment, not gratitude. I'll let a dentist drill into my teeth if I know I need it; if he tries to force me into that chair, I will likely respond with hatred.

Cloud and Townsend wisely warn that "people bring insults and pain on themselves when they confront irresponsible people. In reality, they just need to stop interrupting the Law of Sowing and Reaping in someone's life."[2]

For instance, if your parents tear you apart and shame you, you say, "I'm not visiting you or talking with you until you learn how to treat me with respect." The consequence of their abuse is losing the opportunity to interact with you.

When a coworker is abrasive and dishonest, you don't cover for him or her; you don't make excuses for them; and you insist that they treat you in a professional manner—or else you'll walk away. When your boss asks you why the two of you aren't meeting, you're honest about it.

You've likely read about the need to let addicts reach their low point (without rescuing them) so they finally want to change for themselves. That's the same principle here. You hope that the toxic behavior will make life so uncomfortable for the toxic person that they'll open their hearts and minds to God's conviction and repent.

Jesus tells us in Matthew 6:33 to play aggressive offense, but just a few verses later—in Matthew 7:6—by telling us to avoid offering pearls to a pig, he adds that we will occasionally need to play defense. Offense and defense *combined* can produce a life in which we can be "more than conquerors" (Romans 8:37).

Self-Defense

When dealing with the type of toxic person Jesus likened to a pig, you'll want to play a particular kind of self-defense—guarding your own heart against bitterness and resentment. For me, my best defense in that regard has been twofold: praying for the toxic person and refusing to engage them further. I'm talking to God more and to the toxic person less.

Praying for the welfare of those who oppose us is what Jesus calls us to do: "Bless those who curse you, pray for those who mistreat you" (Luke 6:28). I pray that God will convict them. I pray that they will be so overwhelmed by God's presence that they'll thirst after love and grace instead of anger and malice. I also pray that they will learn how much more pleasing it is to encourage, serve, and build up than to gossip, demean, and tear down. We should all pray for more workers, because Jesus asks us to (Luke 10:2). *Far* better than seeing a toxic person defeated, humiliated, and dismantled is to see them transformed into a loving servant of Christ.

For the kingdom's sake, we should hope for one more faithful worker rather than one less enemy.

What I have also learned to do, however, is to *not* engage them. Here's what you need to know about the psychology and spirituality of toxic people: *they like conflict.* It feeds them. And they have a voracious appetite for it. Toxic people feed off *increasing* conflict, causing more trouble, and attacking more victims. They get a taste and become more rabid. They live for division in the same way a true believer delights in peace.

Engaging them only riles them up and puts their focus on *you*. What I've found is that when you stop playing along, when you're willing to walk away, they have to find another victim. They can't stop being toxic, so they'll find someone else to engage. I guarantee you that if you're being assaulted by a toxic person, you are not the first or only victim. There are probably dozens. One woman whom I had to block on Twitter bragged on Facebook about how many ministries and "well-known" Christians had blocked her. It was a point of *pride* for her.

It may sound selfish to suggest that you should let them go attack someone else, but the fact that they are attacking others isn't your fault. You're not forcing them to attack, and it's not like they'll stop attacking others if they can also attack you. It doesn't work that way. You may merely serve as their dessert. By walking away, you're just being faithful to the important work God has called you to do. And it's just possible that your walking away may be one of the ways that will teach them that they have to eventually change their ways. Dan Allender and Tremper Longman counsel, "One of the greatest gifts one can give a person inclined to evil is the strength to frustrate their attempts to dominate."[3]

The more you understand the psychological makeup and spiritual bent of a toxic person, the quicker you'll be to disengage and, by your silence, let them move on to someone else. Just like Jesus did and tells us to do, learn how to play defense and *walk away*.

Takeaways

- The Bible calls us to employ different strategies for different situations. There's no one magic method to employ when serving God.
- In Matthew 7:6, Jesus lays the groundwork for playing defense, recognizing that some people are toxic and need to be avoided. Spiritual "dogs" and "pigs" won't change or appreciate our efforts, but will instead attack us and try to take us down.
- Seeking first the kingdom of God and finding reliable people are such urgent tasks that we may have to employ spiritual triage. Knowing that the time is short and our time and energy are limited, we seek to focus on the most fertile fields.

- If a person displays no conviction, we should think twice about offering counsel. It's about working *with* God instead of just *for* God.
- Instead of trying to convince a toxic person to leave their ways, we can allow "the law of sowing and reaping" to soften their hearts.
- Because toxic people have a thirst to attack, engaging them energizes them, so it's best to step away and let them focus on someone else.
- As you step away, pray for the toxic individual. For the sake of the kingdom, it's better to have one more newly repentant worker than one less enemy. Stepping away from a toxic person doesn't mean you hate them or don't care about them; it just means you choose to not interact with them.

CHAPTER 9

LOVE TELLS
THE TRUTH

Aaron was beside himself working for a difficult boss, wanting to represent Christ to a troubled (and clearly toxic) individual, wanting to keep his income but also wanting to maintain his sanity. It was becoming increasingly difficult to manage all three aims.

When his counselor finally said, "You know your boss is toxic, right? This is *abusive* behavior, exhibited not just toward you but also others in your office," Aaron felt like a light had been turned on that helped him see the situation with a new clarity. His recent history finally made sense. Of course the workplace was difficult! And no, he *couldn't* "fix" it. You can't have a healthy, non-difficult relationship with a toxic person. So for Aaron, applying the "toxic" label wasn't about demeaning his boss. Rather, it was about understanding why he felt like he was going crazy at times, adjusting his expectations and realigning his strategies to honor God in a difficult situation.

Labels can be hurtful when they are used to attack, but sometimes they can lead to healing when used with discretion. In this case, labeling his boss helped Aaron understand his past, reset his expectations, and lay out more effective strategies for the future.

A similar experience happened to Alicia. She had been to many marriage conferences (with and without her husband) and read many marriage books but still couldn't understand why nothing "worked." She doubled down with prayer and humility, all the while feeling like a failure as a wife. She thought she just needed to find that one magic strategy and then, finally, her marriage could be healed.

When Alicia read Leslie Vernick's *The Emotionally Destructive*

Marriage, her marital experience finally made sense.[1] She wasn't crazy. She was married to an abusive, gaslighting husband. The problem was that she had been receiving good advice for healthy couples, but bad advice for women married to abusive men. A new label helped her understand how to reevaluate her future and what she was doing.

In an entirely different scenario with a different marriage, Tim felt beaten up by the church. His marriage seemed so distant, and the default position in many evangelical circles is that the husband is always to blame. Tim did an amazing share of the household chores, though his wife didn't work outside the home. He was very involved in his kids' lives and was far more likely to be the one who put them to bed. He initiated "God talk" with his family, was faithful taking them all to church, and went out of his way to spoil his wife on birthdays and anniversaries and give her random surprise presents.

His wife discounted all of this because she thought Tim had just one agenda—more sex. Part of this was true. Tim did want sexual intimacy more than once a month. But he laid down a pattern of consistent care for years without his wife even considering the need to raise the frequency of intimate relations. His loving care obviously wasn't tied to results because the results were abysmal, yet Tim kept loving and caring nevertheless.

When Tim talked to friends, pastors, and even counselors, their default position was to assume Tim wasn't doing his share of the housework (leaving his wife too tired), wasn't doing enough non-sexual touch and affirmation to get his wife ready, and was generally failing as a husband. Tim thought he was going to go crazy. He believed he was already doing all three of those and didn't understand how he could possibly do more.

It wasn't until another married couple who had the opportunity to view both Tim and his wife in various situations told him, "Tim, you're married to a very selfish and manipulative woman," that he felt like he regained his sanity. The wife had seen all that had been going on; she had even tried to gently challenge Tim's wife. For instance, she knew Tim's wife spent several hours a day on Facebook and Instagram and liked having the power over Tim that regularly saying no to sex gave her. Her lack of interest wasn't about a lack of time; it was about indifference, selfishness, and manipulation.

A married couple speaking the truth and affirming Tim turned the light on in his mind: "You can't do more than you've already done, Tim. No husband could. No husband is perfect, but you're loving and serving her about as well as any wife in the church is being loved and served. This isn't about you. It's about her."

Understanding the truth is the doorway to new life. And understanding the truth often requires the use of labels. Honoring someone, whether that person is a boss, parent, or spouse, doesn't mean we have to pretend they're something they're not. Honoring and honesty can exist side by side.

Jesus Used Labels

The gospels recount plenty of occasions (beyond the "pigs and pearls" passage we just studied) where Jesus boldly called toxic people toxic—at least "conceptually" (the contemporary word *toxic* doesn't have a counterpart in ancient Greek).

You may recall that Jesus called Herod a "fox" in Luke 13:32. Back in the seventies when my hair was long and feathered and I was wearing Star jeans and clogs, if a young woman called me a fox, I would have basked in the praise *for days*. But a fox in the first century was considered a nasty vermin.

Jesus warned his disciples, "'Be careful. Watch out for the yeast of the Pharisees and that of Herod" (Mark 8:15). Jesus thought it was both necessary and helpful to warn his followers against the toxicity of this group. If you know someone is doing great damage, it's not "kind" to ignore it or pretend they're "good people" with a different point of view. In fact, overlooking toxicity can be cruel to the future victims you fail to warn.

Early on in his ministry, Jesus called out Judas, telling the disciples, "Have I not chosen you, the Twelve? Yet one of you is a devil!" (John 6:70).

Jesus "labeled" the Pharisees during his famous "Seven Woes" teachings in Matthew 23, accusing them of traveling over "land and sea" to make a convert but when doing so they were making them "twice as much a child of hell as you are" (verse 15). He further calls them "blind fools" (verse 17), "hypocrites" (verse 23), "blind guides" (verse 24), and "snakes" (verse 33).

The apostle Paul followed his Savior's example. Paul confronted a sorcerer who was attempting to keep an intelligent and earnest proconsul named Sergius from the faith. "Paul, filled with the Holy Spirit, looked straight at Elymas and said, 'You are a child of the devil and an enemy of everything that is right! You are full of all kinds of deceit and trickery. Will you never stop perverting the right ways of the Lord?'" (Acts 13:9–10).

Jesus and Paul obviously didn't believe that dismissing someone's evil and sin as "well-intentioned but misguided" is always the right path. They called people out on their toxicity, and it wasn't mean for them to do so. That's because there's a difference between labeling and name-calling.

Labeling Isn't Name-Calling

One of the reasons we may be so reluctant to label people is that we rightfully think of name-calling as mean. But labeling isn't name-calling. I'm not suggesting that Aaron dismiss his boss by loudly shouting so the whole office can hear, "You're toxic!" I don't think Tim's marriage will be healed by him saying to his wife, "Drew and Mandy both think you're selfish and manipulative."

Name-calling is about hurting, demeaning, and using words as a weapon. Labeling is about understanding. It's helpful, in one sense, for Tim to know his wife is selfish and manipulative because what works for a "healthy" wife may not work for his wife. Aaron needs to adjust his strategy in working for a toxic boss, because appealing to reason and good manners won't get him very far, as it would with a healthy boss. Alicia may have to learn how to not blame herself for her husband's behavior. Labels can heal and point the way forward.

When I'm in a toxic situation, I change my tactics. I don't expect the other person to act in a nontoxic way. That just leads to disappointment. Instead, I am focused on speaking the truth, guarding my sanity (trying to understand crazy behavior just makes you crazy), and doubling down on prayer: "Heavenly Father, how do I best honor and serve you in this situation?" In a later chapter, "Living and Working with Judas," we'll offer more practical, detailed advice for handling a toxic person in a situation where you can't just walk away.

For now let me just state that when interacting with a toxic person I have two aims: I want to *do the right thing*—keep seeking first God's kingdom—and *be the right person*—nontoxic in return and acting out of love (whether that leads to confrontation or walking away depends on the situation). I can't control a toxic person. I can't change a toxic person. I can't understand a toxic person. *But I can guard my mission and maintain my character.* Those are the only two things you control when you live or work around toxic people. And that's what labeling is all about—helping you hold up your end of the interaction.

The Sin of Detraction

A caveat here: we should be wary of labeling someone too quickly. A biblical counselor told me that some wives will come into a counseling session armed with a list of *DSM-5*[1] categories and plop those labels on their husbands: "He's a narcissist."

Most of us (especially including myself here) aren't qualified to make professional diagnoses. Don't be too quick to apply the "toxic" label and thereby dismiss someone just because you find them uncomfortable or not to your liking. You could be missing an opportunity for your own weakness, fears, insecurities, or sins to be exposed in healthy Christian community, in which we all have different personalities and styles of relating. *Just because somebody bugs you doesn't make them toxic.* God creates both forceful people and accommodating people; it's a sin to think others are in sin just because they have a different style of relating to others than you do. That's pride. That's making yourself the standard everyone should follow rather than Jesus.

But there have been times in my life when applying a label

---

1. The American Psychiatric Association's *Diagnostic and Statistical Manual of Mental Disorders*, 5th ed., is the most accepted guidebook for mental health professionals and counselors to diagnose mental disorders.

brought light, understanding, hope, and healing. Here's how you know the difference: the fruit of labeling is positive; you're trying to serve God and function in a way that honors fellowship and community while maintaining your character. The motivation is love—to serve God and serve others with a right spirit. We're not seeking to *harm*; we're seeking to *understand* and discern how best to serve God.

The fruit of name-calling is destructive. It's about destroying someone's reputation. I should never call someone toxic to hurt them or injure their reputation with others. That's name-calling.

"Detraction" isn't talked about much these days, but it's a great sin. The ancients described it as purposefully trying to lessen someone's reputation. Louis of Granada (writing in the sixteenth century) tells us this has been a big sin for a long time: "The abominable sin of detraction is so prevalent at the present day that there is scarcely a society, a family, an individual not guilty of it. There are some persons so perversely inclined that they cannot bear to hear any good of another, but are always alive to their neighbor's faults, always ready to tear his character to pieces."[2]

The reason detraction is so evil is that it "consists in the threefold injury which it inflicts—namely, on the one who speaks, on him who listens with approval, and on the victim who is assailed in his absence."[3]

One sin but three casualties! A solid church or small group can be torn apart in weeks if detraction goes unchecked. We shouldn't participate in detraction by speaking it *or* by listening to it. It would grieve me greatly if people used this book to attack others rather than preserve their own mission.

In the midst of necessary labeling—in which we may want to seek out qualified counsel with mature believers to understand what's going on—we must never resort to hateful name-calling or detraction.

Louis of Granada's words should be well-heeded: "Henceforward consider your neighbor's character as a forbidden tree which you cannot touch. Be no less slow in praising yourself than in censuring others, for the first indicates vanity and the second a want of charity. Speak of the virtues of your neighbor, but be silent as to his faults."[4]

Having said this, if you are counseling (formally or informally) someone who is dealing with a toxic person, you have to call a toxic person toxic. Doing so is *not* the sin of detraction. In the words of Francis de Sales, "We must not, in order to avoid the vice of detraction, favor, flatter, or cherish vice; but we must openly and freely speak of evil, and blame that which is blamable . . . It is charity to cry out against the wolf, wherever he is, more especially when he is among the sheep."[5]

You won't help anyone by pretending a toxic person isn't toxic, or dismissing valid concerns. You can't learn to handle a toxic person by pretending she or he is healthy. Discussing in a redemptive way how to maintain your mission and character in the face of a toxic influence isn't gossip—that's community. Gossiping about someone or talking about someone just to vent—that's the sin of detraction, and it needs to be shunned. Warning someone about a toxic personality is one thing; telling someone else about a toxic person (who doesn't have any reason to be warned) just to talk, have something interesting to say, or belittle the toxic person is sin.

Dr. Steve Wilke explains gossip in a simple, understandable way: "Gossip is when you talk to someone about somebody else when they are not part of the problem or solution."[6]

Labels have a place—to heal and to strategize. Never use labels to attack or tear down.

Takeaways

- In the interest of your own sanity and ministry effectiveness, it can be helpful to learn how to apply labels. If you don't understand what you're facing, you won't be able to come up with a redemptive strategy.
- Jesus and Paul both used labels to describe others.
- Labeling is distinguished from name-calling in that labeling seeks to understand, while name-calling seeks to harm.
- While acknowledging the need to use labels, we should do so humbly. Detraction is a serious sin to be avoided.

CHAPTER 10

A MAN WITH A MISSION

If only Satan were lazy.

He's got just about every other evil cornered, excelling at the worst of the worst. It would be so convenient if he also tended toward sloth, but alas, he does not.

Not even close.

Nor do his followers apparently.

To be given a mission from God is to be surrounded by many aggressive opponents and hyperactive enemies. Their attacks are clever, creative, and varied. Toxic people use blatant aggression and passive aggression. They pretend to be our friends, and then when that doesn't work, they threaten us as enemies. They act like they want to protect us and then try to control us. They hit from the left, and when that is blocked, they will come at us from the right.

Keep in mind, merely distracting you is a win for them. If they can't ultimately *defeat* your work, they at least want to *delay* your work.

Our job, based on Matthew 6:33 and 2 Timothy 2:2, requires us to maintain a laser-sharp focus with wisdom, discernment, and determination.

One of the all-time best conquerors of a pervasive toxic attack is Nehemiah, who in the fifth century BC was called by God to rebuild the walls of Jerusalem. Nehemiah's deft and brilliant handling of the toxic people who opposed him lays out a wise, spiritually sensitive pattern for dealing with malicious adversaries.

The Call

In case you don't know the backstory, Jehoiakim, the king of Judah, rebelled against Nebuchadnezzar, the king of Babylon, in 586 BC—with disastrous results. Babylon's army destroyed Jerusalem and reduced its famous temple to ashes. Not quite fifty years later, Cyrus of Persia defeated the Babylonians and gained control of what had been Jerusalem. He gave the Jewish people permission to return to the city site in 536, and a newer, smaller version of the temple was rebuilt and dedicated in 516.

Rebuilding an "economy version" of the temple was a small, largely religious gesture that didn't create much friction or attention from the surrounding people. Jerusalem was still sparsely populated, a tiny outpost at best. Ezra sought to change this and led fifteen hundred men and their families to resettle and essentially repopulate Jerusalem in 455 BC.

About a year later, Nehemiah, cupbearer to King Artaxerxes, sought and received permission to leave the king's presence and rebuild Jerusalem's wall. Though rebuilding the temple hadn't stirred up any enemies, Nehemiah's determination to rebuild Jerusalem's wall unleashed vicious and murderous toxic attacks.

The natural question to ask is *"why?"* Why was rebuilding the *wall* (as opposed to the temple, which had been completed sixty years prior) so significant?

The temple had religious significance, which wasn't a particular threat to the Persians, but a wall around Jerusalem had *political* significance. It was a *civic* statement as much as it was a *religious* one. That's why it required the permission of the ruling king, which Nehemiah received from Artaxerxes.

One of the lessons from this is that civic leaders, doing civic work, are "seeking first the kingdom of God" every bit as much as religious workers. If God is behind your effort, and God is your motivating influence, and God is the one you're seeking to please, you are indeed seeking first his kingdom, even if it's not church-related. Civic change can actually be more threatening to some toxic opponents than religious reformation. As long as you "keep it within the walls of the church," they're fine. Act like God wants to influence society? You better stay alert.

Stop!

As will be the case with many true works of God, toxic individuals rose up with a feverish passion to stop Nehemiah, asking him for a meeting: "Sanballat and Geshem sent me this message: 'Come, let us meet together in one of the villages on the plain of Ono'" (Nehemiah 6:2).

Toxic people may sound reasonable. How could Nehemiah refuse a meeting? After all, aren't God's followers called to reach out to others? What could be wrong with getting together for a chat?

Mission-minded people don't have time for sentimental foolishness. Nehemiah saw through the facade to these men's real intentions and refused the meeting. Here's why:

> But they were scheming to harm me; so I sent messengers to them with this reply: "I am carrying on a great project and cannot go down. Why should the work stop while I leave it and go down to you?" Four times they sent me the same message, and each time I gave them the same answer.
>
> NEHEMIAH 6:2–4

Nehemiah recognizes this entreaty as a distracting toxic attack, not a good-faith effort. He lives in the truth and applies discernment. A senseless meeting isn't worthy of his time. Rather than wasting effort getting into a silly spat, he puts it in utilitarian terms, essentially saying, "I'm too busy to be distracted by you."

The toxic enemies are persistent. They live to wreak havoc. Instead of finding purpose and focus by seeking the kingdom on their own, they spend their time attacking others who are building the kingdom. They rarely take no for an answer, as we see here. They follow up with three additional appeals, trying to wear Nehemiah down.

This is a warning worth heeding. I'm ashamed to admit that I'm personally particularly weak when this happens to me. I can tell somebody no once, sometimes with a lame excuse, and when I'm at my best perhaps I'll say no twice, but I usually buckle the third or fourth time, out of false guilt and a prideful, people-pleasing attitude.

Not Nehemiah!

He stays true to his work and call. Sanballat responds to Nehemiah's final refusal by resorting to threats:

> Then, the fifth time [how *annoying!*], Sanballat sent his aide to me with the same message, and in his hand was an unsealed letter in which was written:
>
> "It is reported among the nations—and Geshem says it is true—that you and the Jews are plotting to revolt, and therefore you are building the wall. Moreover, according to these reports you are about to become their king and have even appointed prophets to make this proclamation about you in Jerusalem: 'There is a king in Judah!' Now this report will get back to the king; so come, let us meet together."
>
> NEHEMIAH 6:5–7

First, the request was for a "reasonable" meeting. Then it escalated into a threat—*and we have a witness!* "If you don't do what we want you to do, the wrong people are going to hear about this—and you'll surely pay."

As if Nehemiah was doing something *wrong*.

When a toxic person doesn't get his or her way, their next gambit is often to make your motives sound sinister. They will lie to others about why you won't meet. They will insist you stop what you're doing and interact with them or else *pay the price*. They will seek to enlist others to pressure you. Toxic people often excel at recruiting others in their distracting wars when they can't distract you one-on-one.

Why do they care? You're their mission! You're seeking first God's kingdom; they're seeking first to distract you. I know it doesn't make much sense. But you'll drive yourself *crazy* trying to make sense out of toxic attacks. They *don't* make sense. They are petty and small-minded. If everyone devoted themselves to seeking first God's kingdom, we wouldn't have the motivation or time to devote ourselves to toxic attacks against others.

Alecia[1] experienced this "distracting" dynamic in a relationship with a coworker named Jennifer. The coworker deluged Alecia with pleas for personal help regarding issues outside the office. As a believer, Alecia did all she could to help, but she soon realized that things were getting out of hand. She wasn't able to help Jennifer, and Jennifer's entreaties were getting in the way of Alecia's own work. As Alecia tried to pull back, Jennifer charged forward, sending Alecia six-page, single-spaced emails and eleven-minute phone messages. If they weren't answered *immediately*, there'd be a sob story about how hurt Jennifer was that Alecia wasn't there for her when Jennifer needed her.

Soon Alecia was worn out and couldn't get her work done. She spent as much time trying to avoid Jennifer as she did focusing on her own responsibilities.

Here's a warning: we Christians often feel guilty for getting worn out with someone, assuming we're just being selfish, but getting worn out handling toxicity makes us weaker and more distracted in our call to fulfill God's mission for our lives.

Alecia finally did what healthy people do—she established some boundaries.

"Jennifer," she said, "we're not going to have personal conversations any more. Let's keep our communication on a professional basis."

Any healthy person would see this as a reasonable request in the workplace and comply.

Not Jennifer.

A few days later, other coworkers started approaching Alecia with "concerned" inquiries about how she could be so unfair to Jennifer.

"Jennifer was so hurt, Alecia. She feels like you've abandoned

---

1. Not her real name.

her, and she doesn't know what she's done wrong. And you won't talk to her about it."

Alecia was beside herself and wanted a pastor's advice.

"Alecia," I asked, "how do they know you don't want to have long personal conversations with Jennifer? Did you tell them?"

"No."

"Did they overhear you talking to her?"

"No."

"So the only way they know is that Jennifer gossiped to them."

Most people get that *gossip* is toxic. My use of that word was deliberate, as it appeared to me that Jennifer was being clever and sly. In fact, she *did* know what she had done wrong. Alecia had been clear and professional. Jennifer just didn't like Alecia's *conclusion*, and like toxic people do, she tried to make everything sound unclear and muddled as she gossiped about Alecia behind her back.

Alecia needed to understand that Jennifer was *still* being toxic. She aimed to control Alecia's time and attention. It was a clever attack—enlist others to make Alecia feel like she's not acting like a believer—but it was still an attack, and Alecia needed to treat it accordingly.

"Just say, 'Listen, it's obvious Jennifer has talked to you about this because I haven't. Who's acting like the Christian here? Does the Bible tell us to go behind someone's back when we don't get our way? And why are you listening to gossip?'"

I then urged her to rely on her reputation in the face of this recent attack. "Ask them, 'Do I seem malicious in any other relationship? Have you found me to be uncaring?'"

Here's the blatant trap you need to be wary of. Some people will want to waste your time and drain you by using a false sense of neediness. When that stops working, they don't give up. If they can't make you sympathize, they'll seek to make you defensive. They'll attack so you'll want to defend yourself. What's going on is that they just want your attention. They want to keep controlling a slice of your time, effort, and energy. Whether you sympathize with them or are angry with them doesn't matter as much as the fact that you notice them and spend time interacting with them.

As we saw earlier, it's really all about control. Again, it doesn't always make sense. It seems ridiculous that someone else would make it their mission to distract you from your mission, but that's what toxic people do.

I didn't understand this earlier in my ministry. I wanted to help everyone. When I realized I was in over my head on certain occasions and tried to pull back (I'm not a trained counselor or professional theologian and have many limitations on my intellect and understanding), the toxic people figured out, "I can still have a relationship with him if I attack him, because he'll respond to that."

It's a sick and disturbing relationship, but to them, *it's still a relationship*—and as a toxic person, they kind of enjoy it.

Don't fall for this trap. Keep your eyes opened to the warped and twisted attack Sanballat was waging against Nehemiah. No reasonable person would believe that Nehemiah was doing what he was doing to proclaim himself king. Toxic people lack real mission, so they create false missions.

Nehemiah was motivated by love, faith, and obedience. Toxic people are motivated by selfishness, hatred, and conflict. You can't win when you're interacting with them because *you're playing entirely different games*. The rules aren't even the same. So do what Nehemiah did:

> I sent him this reply: "Nothing like what you are saying is happening; you are just making it up out of your head."
>
> They were all trying to frighten us, thinking, "Their hands will get too weak for the work, and it will not be completed."
>
> But I prayed, "Now strengthen my hands."
>
> NEHEMIAH 6:8–9

When people distract you from your mission to God, find refuge in God: "Now strengthen my hands." Instead of talking to them or wasting your time with them, double down on prayer. Get God's heart, courage, comfort, and affirmation. Why waste time trying to placate a toxic person (as if you could stop their hatred anyway) when you could spend time receiving love and instruction from the God of the universe?

One of the best defenses against toxic attacks, then, is seeking what John Climacus called true meekness, "a permanent condition of that soul which remains unaffected by whether or not it is spoken well of, whether or not it is honored or praised."[1] As we'll see at the end of this chapter, the goal is a soul oriented around God's approval, entirely free from either toxic assaults or empty flattery. We have one boss—our heavenly Father—and our focus should be on pleasing *him*, wanting to hear *him* say, "Well done, good and faithful servant!" (Matthew 25:21).

Why Can't We Be Friends?

Pleas didn't work with Nehemiah. Threats didn't work either. So his enemies pretended to be friends who wanted to "protect" him from others: "One day I went to the house of Shemaiah . . . who was shut in at his home. He said, 'Let us meet in the house of God, inside the temple, and let us close the temple doors, because men are coming to kill you—by night they are coming to kill you'" (Nehemiah 6:10).

Shemaiah is a religious name, most often given to Levites, prophets, and priests. The context here suggests that this Shemaiah is a prophet. Tobiah and Sanballat went for "religious cover" to distract Nehemiah from his God-given calling. They had warned him of political ramifications ("we're going to tell the king"); Nehemiah didn't fall for it, so now they're bringing in the religious argument: "Surely you'd listen to a prophet . . ."

In order to "protect" himself, however, Nehemiah would have to do what? He'd have to suspend his mission! There's no way this man of God was going to be fooled by that.

> But I said, "Should a man like me run away? Or should someone like me go into the temple to save his life? I will not go!"
> I realized that God had not sent him, but that he had prophesied against me because Tobiah and Sanballat had hired him.

He had been hired to intimidate me so that I would commit a sin by doing this, and then they would give me a bad name to discredit me.

NEHEMIAH 6:11–13

Nehemiah knows he's dealing with clever toxic people, but he doesn't become obsessed with them. That would be yet another trap. Instead, he simply commits them to God. No slander, no gossip, no malice. Just prayer: "Remember Tobiah and Sanballat, my God, because of what they have done; remember also the prophet Noadiah and how she and the rest of the prophets have been trying to intimidate me" (Nehemiah 6:14).

Sadly, "church" people can be just as toxic as non-church people, as demonstrated here by Shemaiah and Noadiah. Nehemiah wisely recognizes that it's not his job to launch a campaign against them or get them unseated. That also would have been a distraction. Best just to pray for them and let God take it from here. After all, they're supposed to represent God in the first place.

Finished

The end result of Nehemiah's focus, determination, and adept handling of toxic opposition is a stunning and stupendous victory: "So the wall was completed on the twenty-fifth of Elul, in fifty-two days" (Nehemiah 6:15).

It's quite extraordinary that Nehemiah and his workers were able to finish the wall around Jerusalem in just fifty-two days. It sparks the question, why wasn't the wall built decades sooner if it could be done in less than two months?

The answer is simple. Prior to Nehemiah, no wise, discerning, mission-minded person was willing to push past the toxic people who were adamant that the wall not be built. Mission-minded people can accomplish a whole lot in a shockingly short amount of time when they stay focused and don't allow toxic people to distract them.

The best way to confound toxic people is to ignore them while you complete the work they want to stop. Serve God faithfully and zealously, and let them commiserate with the devil when their own plans fail.

The Real Witness

Now notice something spiritually spectacular. By not being distracted by the toxic people's pleas, by avoiding their threats, by not being drawn into false entreaties to friendship, Nehemiah served the toxic people more in *resisting them* than he would have by *giving in to them*.

How so?

Nothing puts toxic people back on their heels like watching a godly servant stay true to their calling and accomplish God's work. It's inspiring: "When all our enemies heard about this, all the surrounding nations were afraid and lost their self-confidence, because they realized that this work had been done with the help of our God" (Nehemiah 6:16).

The best thing you can do to witness to a toxic person is stay focused on your task, refuse to be distracted or play their games, pray instead of gossip, and then *get the work done*. Find the reliable people God has called you to invest in. Accomplish the task that you know to be urgent. *Then they will see that God is God, and they are not.* That's the message they most need to hear. That's the best way for you to witness to them. If toxicity works for them, they'll never leave their toxic strategies behind. The best thing you can do for a toxic person who unjustly opposes you is to make sure they fail in distracting you from your God-given mission. Testify to them by means of God-empowered and God-breathed success.

Here's how warped toxic opposition is. When a toxic person directs you and distracts you, they are seeking to become your god with a little "g" (once again, it's about control). They want you to be directed and motivated by them! "I will plead with your good nature; if that doesn't work, I will threaten you; if that doesn't work, I will pretend I'm your friend and try to trick you; I will enlist others, both civic *and* religious authorities, to back me up, but I am determined that you will eventually do what I want you to do!"

A servant of God says in response, "I serve the one true God, not you. I do his will, not yours. I am driven by his mission, not by your attacks. You are not my god, and I will neither serve nor pay attention to you."

This is a lesson toxic people need to learn.

One More Try

One final lesson from Nehemiah: toxic people often refuse to admit defeat. Such was the case with Nehemiah's enemies. Later on in Nehemiah 6, we read, "Tobiah sent letters to intimidate me" (verse 19).

Even after the wall was completed, Tobiah wouldn't let it go, which points out another potential trap: if toxic people can't *stop* your mission, they will set out to *distract* you while you are maintaining your mission.

Your job is to continue to ignore the toxic people and find the reliable ones to invest in. Listen to what the wise Nehemiah did in light of this ongoing attack: "I put in charge of Jerusalem my brother Hanani, along with Hananiah the commander of the citadel, because he was a man of integrity and feared God more than most people do" (Nehemiah 7:2).

Nehemiah had found his "reliable people" qualified to teach others, and that's who he focused on, and so should we. Why waste time arguing with a toxic person who only wants to distract you when you can join forces with someone who fears God more than most people do and advance the work?

The End Result

Nehemiah's faithfulness and skill in handling toxic people resulted in many people praising God. Ezra led a worship service of all Jerusalem's citizens, now meeting behind a secure wall. Here's how Nehemiah describes it: "Ezra praised the LORD, the great God; and all the people lifted their hands and responded, 'Amen! Amen!' Then they bowed down and worshiped the LORD with their faces to the ground" (Nehemiah 8:6).

Instead of trying to make toxic people happy or satisfied (which is a waste of time, since they can't and won't be mollified), *live to help reliable people serve and worship God.* Our job is to open up new avenues of worship with people who want to reverence God. Rather than living to make toxic people feel good about us, *let's live to make reliable people excited about God.*

The book of Nehemiah ends beautifully, even poetically, with a verse that has changed my life focus. After coming to a clear understanding of a problem (Jerusalem exposed, without a wall), accepting the mission to secure it, learning how not to be distracted or defeated by toxic opponents, investing in reliable people to carry on the work, and leading an entire nation into a new season of worship, Nehemiah reveals his heart's true desire: "Remember me with favor, my God" (Nehemiah 13:31).

We will be most helpful to God when we care exclusively about how *God* remembers us and learn not to care about how toxic people view us or talk about us. We have one God—the Creator God—and it is idolatrous to let little "gods" direct us, dissuade us, or even distract us.

When Focus on the Family broadcasts one of my interviews, it's a happy couple of days. Books on Amazon get a big boost. People remember you exist and often post on Twitter or Facebook some nice things about what you said. And everybody is happy.

Well, not everybody.

There's a woman who apparently believes her mission in life is to troll Facebook, find someone who says anything nice about me, and then set them straight about how awful I am, how destructive my books are, and how no one should ever listen to anything I say.

In my weaker moments, I have responded, wanting to explain things to the original person who made the post, helping them understand what's really going on. But then the detractor responds again, and it gets messy.

I once finally signed off by writing to the woman in question: "I'm not going to argue with you. Anyone can see the way you've treated me and how I have never responded in kind but let God be the judge between both of us." In this case, I clearly sensed God telling me to spend my time and energy writing one helpful sentence for a blog or book (investing in reliable people) rather than waste even *ten more seconds* trying to counter her attacks. She feeds off conflict. It's what makes her come alive. And I'm not helping anyone by enabling that.

Most of the time, I listen to God and move on, but I'm weak enough that sometimes I give in and engage again (if you notice me doing that in the future, feel free to refer me back to this chapter).

Nehemiah 13:31 has become my new go-to Scripture for these tempting seasons: "Remember me with favor, my God."

That's all that matters. Not what she thinks about me. Not what others on social media think about me. We should all live to be remembered with favor *by God*. Live to hear your Creator, Lord, and Savior say, "Well done, good and faithful servant" (Matthew 24:21).

Let's learn to focus, fulfill our mission, resist the distractions, and live to be remembered with favor by the one true God.

And that means saying no to the toxic distracters.

Takeaways

- Nehemiah's experience offers a great example of how to complete a task without being distracted by toxic people.
- Seeking first God's kingdom can be a civic work as much as a religious work.
- For whatever reason, toxic people make it their mission to stop or delay other people's mission.
- If seemingly pleasant entreaties don't distract us, toxic people may resort to threats and/or enlist other people to question our motives.
- Two good defenses against toxic distraction include praying to God rather than interacting with the toxic attacks and exhibiting

meekness, a spiritual state in which we aren't motivated by others' praise or assaults.

- When mission-minded people stay focused and undistracted, it's amazing how much and how quickly they can get things done.
- We serve toxic people more by completing our task than by giving in to them. Spiritual success points people back to God and reminds toxic people that they don't get to control us.
- Instead of trying to make toxic people satisfied with us, we should put our efforts into helping reliable people serve and worship God.
- Our best defense against toxic attacks is living to be remembered with favor *by God*.

CHAPTER 11

LOOKING LIKE JESUS WHEN WORKING WITH JUDAS

Sometimes, you can't walk away from toxic people entirely. They may be coworkers, relatives, bosses, church members, neighbors, in-laws, and the like. One man—we'll call him Mike—worked in a contract situation with a clearly toxic man named Joe. Mike describes Joe as a "level 10 narcissist." Bolstered by his enormous business success and possessor of a high intellect, Joe has crafted a world that revolves around him.

Joe has no true friends, and he's been unfaithful to his (now ex-) wife multiple times, so he uses his money as a way to keep people hanging around him by overpaying employees and handing out huge bonuses.

"He will give someone thousands of dollars," Mike says, "but it's all about putting them in his debt. He wants to own you."

The reason Mike can work around Joe without going crazy himself is that (1) he's a very strong individual himself (spiritually and emotionally), and (2) he doesn't seek to control Joe back.

"The only control I have over Joe is how much I limit his control over me. I don't ride the roller coasters with him. If he's super angry, I'm not hurt by his attacks. If he's ecstatically pleased, I don't accept his accolades. He's going to be up and down; I choose to be constant and consistent. He doesn't get to define my mood on any given day."

Joe wants Mike's respect, and he's willing to pay for it. On one occasion, Joe set up an elaborate, prepaid vacation for an employee and her husband. It was an expensive cruise—everything was first class.

The employee balked. She had just had a child; her health wasn't the best; and the schedule didn't suit her husband's employment situation.

"I've already paid for it," Joe responded. "You're going to go."

What she didn't know, and what Mike knew, is that she was about to be subpoenaed to testify against Joe, and Joe was determined to keep her out of the country so she couldn't be served. The employee's husband put his foot down—they *weren't* going on the cruise. So Joe, knowing the employee's doctor, went to her physician, said he was concerned about her health, and had the doctor order her to six weeks of bed rest—a carefully calculated plot to keep her out of the office.

Joe was bragging about how he had paid for the (unused) cruise, how he was covering her "bed rest," and what an exemplary boss he was, but in private, Mike would have none of it. "You're manipulating her," he said. "This isn't about her health; it's about controlling your legal problems, and you're making her an acceptable expense."

Mike's opinion mattered to Joe, so Joe launched a plan to win him over. He showed up at lunch one day and said, "I made reservations at this great steak house."

"I can't leave," Mike said.

"Come on, it'll be the best lunch you've ever had."

"Sorry, Joe, but I've got other plans."

Joe handed Mike a box.

"What's this?"

"Just open it after I'm gone."

Mike opened it up and counted five thousand dollars in cash. He called Joe, and Joe said, "Ah, you opened it. So, we're good now, you and me?"

"No. I still think you're acting like a jerk. You come pick up this cash, or I'm giving it to your ex-wife [whom Joe was divorcing]."

"Don't do that! I'll be right over."

Mike survives working around Joe by understanding how Joe

is motivated, and through his own integrity, Mike sidesteps being owned.

"Joe has constructed the perfect universe of people who owe him, so I make sure I'm not in that universe. If you enter that universe, Joe has two options for you—he'll do anything to *gain your loyalty*, but if you won't give him that, he'll do anything he can to *ruin you*. I'm established enough in my other businesses where he can't ruin me, and he knows that."

When we *can* walk away from toxic people, we probably and usually should. But when financial necessity, work obligations, family relationships, or even the accomplishment of our God-given mission necessitates that we find a way to live or work with a toxic person, we can learn much by following Jesus' example with Judas.

Jesus and Judas

Though Jesus often walked away and let others walk away, he obviously and clearly kept one toxic person very close to his side—his betrayer, Judas. Let's focus on three key strategies, based on Jesus' interaction with Judas, for how we can live with or work alongside toxic people without going crazy ourselves.

Jesus Didn't View His Mission as Stopping Toxic People from Sinning

Maybe it seems more obvious to you, but it was startling to me when I realized Jesus knew Judas was a thief and never chose to stop him. John clues us in: "One of [Jesus'] disciples, Judas Iscariot, who was later to betray him, objected, 'Why wasn't this perfume sold and the money given to the poor? It was worth a year's wages.' He did not say this because he cared about the poor but because he was a thief; as keeper of the money bag, he used to help himself to what was put into it" (John 12:4–6).

If John knew Judas was a thief, *Jesus* knew Judas was a thief. In fact, Jesus knew that Judas was worse than a thief. In John 6:70, Jesus said, "'Have I not chosen you, the Twelve? Yet one of you is a devil!' (He meant Judas, the son of Simon Iscariot, who, though one of the Twelve, was later to betray him.)" Jesus knew Judas was toxic. He could have stopped Judas from stealing and his future betrayal by kicking him out of their group at any time.

But he didn't.

Why?

Jesus kept the bigger mission in mind. To seek first God's kingdom, he had to raise up a band of disciples. He also had to die on the cross. He wasn't waylaid by individual battles of piety with his disciples, as we are prone to do with people around us. Addressing Judas's thievery would be like a neurosurgeon clipping someone's fingernails. There were more important issues at hand. And Jesus' mission was not to stop everybody from sinning.

This is actually a freeing word for believers. Your mission is not to confront every sin you hear or know of, even among your perhaps toxic family members or coworkers. Of course, if you're a parent of a child still living at home, confronting sin is an appropriate part of spiritual training. But at extended family gatherings, with hard-hearted friends and certainly coworkers, our job isn't to be "sin detectives" who discover how others are messing up and then unleash havoc by sharing our opinions with those who don't want to hear them.

Jesus could have spent all twenty-four hours of every day trying to confront every one of his disciples' sins. "Peter, put away that anger!" "Thomas, you're still doubting me, aren't you?" "Thaddeus, you're people-pleasing again. Nobody likes a suck-up."

Instead, he focused on training and equipping reliable people. Focusing on others' sin makes you focus on what's toxic. Focusing on *training* makes you focus on what is good and on who is reliable. The latter is a much more enjoyable and ultimately much more productive life.

Because our goal is to seek first God's kingdom and righteousness, and to seek out reliable people in the process, we've got to let a few things slide right by us. That uncle who brings another woman half his age to Thanksgiving dinner? Not our problem. The coworker who had too much to drink at the office party? If we're not the boss, that's not our concern. Besides, one sin is never the issue. Alienation from God, shattered psyches, unhealed and unaddressed hurts—those are the real issues.

Feel free to enjoy people and love them without having to serve as their conscience. When asked sincerely, speak the truth, as Mike did to Joe. Just know that merely witnessing sin in your presence doesn't require you to act as prosecuting attorney, judge, and jury. Mike, whom we mentioned earlier, has a full life, his own business, and a family with kids still living at home, not to mention his work at church. If he made it his life goal to point out every one of Joe's "sins," he'd never get anything else done, and working with Joe would become untenable.

Keep the bigger picture in mind. Instead of upending the holiday gathering by making sure everyone knows you disapprove of what that child, cousin, uncle, or parent is doing, find a hungry soul to quietly encourage, bless, inspire, and challenge. Find the most "reliable" relative and invest in them.

Jesus Didn't Let Judas's Toxicity Become His

How much money would you spend to get an hour to ask Jesus all the questions you've ever wanted to ask him?

What would it be worth to you to go back to the first century and spend an entire weekend with Jesus, watching him perform miracles, listening to his teachings, participating in private conversations, watching him pray and interact with others?

I'm guessing, if you're reading a book like this, a whole lot.

All of which makes Judas's betrayal seem all the more ungrateful. Jesus gave him a front-row seat to the most significant life ever lived, and Judas sold him out.

And yet at the Last Supper, when Jesus washed his disciples' feet, Jesus made sure that Judas was still present. In a picture the sheer wonder of which leaves me in awe, Jesus used the two holiest hands that have ever existed, the two most precious hands in the history of humankind, the hands pierced for our salvation—Jesus took *those* exquisite hands and washed the feet of his toxic betrayer.

Even in the face of ungratefulness and malice, Jesus kept the door open to relational reconciliation. He loved Judas to the end, essentially saying, "You can't make me hate you. Your toxicity won't become my toxicity."

Just as astonishing to me is what happened during the act of betrayal. When Judas walks up to Jesus to hand him over to the soldiers, Jesus looks at Judas and says, "Do what you came for, friend" (Matthew 26:50).

Friend?

How about *skunk*? How about *snake*?

Jesus said "friend" because Jesus didn't have a toxic molecule in his body. There was nowhere for toxicity to take root.

God is radically *for* people. He wants everyone to come to a knowledge of the truth (1 Timothy 2:4). As his followers, we also must be for everyone, even if we oppose what they're doing. If we must live and work with toxic people, our call is to make sure their toxicity doesn't become ours. We don't treat them as they treat us. We don't offer evil in exchange for evil. We love. We serve. We guard our hearts so that we are not poisoned by their bad example.

In her mid-thirties, Nicole works in an industry that has not been kind to women.[1] It's beginning to change because it must, but Nicole is still a bit of a pioneer in having to deal with the "not yet" part. She believes she has been marginalized in part for being a woman, and some of her male coworkers' responses sound flat-out misogynistic to me. When she called out a male coworker for making a mistake that cost the company hundreds of thousands of dollars, he asked her if she was upset because it was her "time of the month."

Why does Nicole stay? As a strong believer, she is convinced this is God's call on her life. "I couldn't handle the toxicity I face if I wasn't absolutely certain of who I am in Christ. In fact, my being a Christian may draw as much ridicule from some coworkers as the fact that I'm

---

1. Some readers may naturally wonder what industry Nicole is in, but for reasons of anonymity, she has asked me not to share any further details. I'm grateful for her testimony and want to honor her trust.

a woman. They think of Christians as ignorant, anti-science, weak do-gooders."

Nicole has a much younger sister, and she wants to set an example for her. "If I left my job every time somebody said something misogynistic or anti-Christian, the toxic people would win. If I lose my seat at the table, I lose influence, and I've come to believe that would be selfish. The younger women and other Christians will have to suffer and fight that battle. My accomplishments have given me a measure of respect with the CEO, so I'm not as easy to push around as someone who is just coming up and is still unproven. But do I have to put up with a lot? Yeah, I do."

Nicole works hard to not allow a poisonous atmosphere to poison her own soul. She prays for her coworkers. She may call a friend in the middle of the day to have a "healthy, edifying" conversation instead of fretting about heated comments in the boardroom. She'll listen to a podcast. She remembers that God's work is moving forward; he's touching many lives; and he has placed Nicole to be a light in a sometimes dark place. Her mission in life isn't to fight the toxic coworkers; it's to complete her mission and guard her own soul in the process.

What Nicole and Mike share in common is an *inner strength*. Nicole isn't afraid to stand up for herself. "When you're dealing with powerful people like our CEO, you have to know that you're supposed to contribute. That's why you're there. You don't allow other colleagues to define you or limit you. And you keep the focus. My job isn't to make the workplace better for women; ultimately, my job is to succeed at what I'm paid to do, and that, indirectly, is what will help other women who follow along.

"I remind myself that every platform I've been given is a trust from God. It's not by accident, and I need to be a good steward. God put me here for a reason, and one thing I've learned about dealing with toxic people is that *it gets easier*. You're not so afraid anymore when you've already lived through it a few times. You know how it ends. In a way, it's almost like a workout. You become stronger. You can lift heavier weights, do cardio longer."

Nicole's faith keeps her grounded. "Few people know how to relate in a healthy way to a very powerful and successful CEO. They can be crushed trying to read between the lines when he makes a comment, or crushed by him not commenting at all. I've just determined that he doesn't get that role in my life. I'm settled in who I am as God's daughter. I don't need another father to affirm me or validate me. Ultimately, my work will validate my employment. I can control my work; I can't control how others spin it.

"And frankly, though this isn't always true, I've found that the most forceful bullies are usually the most insecure. I often pity them as much as I'm disgusted by them. I know that if they're speaking to me the way they do, they can't have an intimate marriage—they can't have a happy life. There's too much insecurity, jealousy, pettiness, and raunchiness in their soul for them to be happy. It must be painful for them to look in the mirror occasionally and admit what they've become.

"So I'm not going to let a person like that who is ruining their own life also ruin mine. I'm not going to let them determine where I work. If the entire office was toxic and it was impacting my health and my own family, I'd probably leave. But I can handle a few toxic individuals. You have to in order to be in this business."

Nicole has learned how to maintain her job *and her character*, just as Jesus did with Judas.

Jesus Spoke Truth to Crazy

While Jesus invited Judas back into relationship until the very moment of betrayal, washing his feet and even calling him friend, he never pretended that what Judas was doing wasn't toxic. In fact, he warned Judas at the Last Supper that if he were to go through with his plans, things wouldn't end well for him: "Woe to that man who betrays the Son of Man! It would be better for him if he had not been born" (Mark 14:21).

When Judas kissed him in Gethsemane, Jesus replied, "Are you betraying the Son of Man with a kiss?" (Luke 22:48).

When working around toxic people, you don't have to pretend

they're not toxic. You don't have to pretend they are well-meaning but perhaps misguided.

The reason this is good news is that it helps preserve our sanity. Toxic people are experts at twisting things, making us feel crazy for admitting the truth (what counselors call gaslighting). But as followers of Jesus, we are committed to the truth because we are committed to Jesus, who said, "I am the way and the *truth* and the life . . ." (John 14:6, emphasis added).

Without truth as a refuge, interacting with crazy people can start to make you feel crazy. But God is a God of order. Craziness is a clear sign of toxicity.

Remember how Mike stood up to Joe? Joe seemed desperate to get Mike's approval, either by bribery or threat. Mike stood firm: "You're manipulating her. Nothing you say or do can change my mind or get me to pretend otherwise."

Mike doesn't call out everything Joe does as wrong. But when asked directly, he *never* pretends everything is fine when it's not. He refuses to try to make sense out of nonsense, or good intentions out of manipulation.

This will sound like such a cliché, but I've found that extra praying brings some level of sanity to a situation that feels crazy. There's something about spending time talking to and listening to the God of truth that restores sanity when you're forced to spend time in a place that makes you feel like you're losing your mind.

As we trust that God understands all that is truly going on, and as we remember that God is the only one capable of bringing everything to account, we can rest in his understanding, promise, and protection: "Do not be anxious about anything, but in every situation, by prayer and petition, with thanksgiving, present your requests to God. And the peace of God, which transcends all understanding, will guard your hearts and your minds in Christ Jesus" (Philippians 4:6–7).

Takeaways

- Sometimes we can't walk away but have to learn how to live or work around toxic people. This will require us to become stronger than we've ever been before.
- Don't try to control a controller. Work around them as you are required to, but don't let their ups and downs become your ups and downs. Keep a healthy level of distance between the two of you.
- Keep first things first. Our job isn't to stop people from sinning. Focus on investing in reliable people.
- Guard against letting someone else's toxicity tempt you to respond in a similarly toxic fashion. We can't control what toxic people do and say, but we can control what *we* do and say.
- Nicole reminds us that you may have to work with or for a toxic person, but you don't have to allow them to validate you. You can be self-motivated by knowing who you are in Christ.
- Don't allow someone who is ruining their life to ruin yours as well. Leave work at work (or family drama at family gatherings).
- Thank God that we never have to pretend crazy isn't crazy. We live by the truth. We don't have to pretend toxic people aren't toxic; we just have to learn a nontoxic way of interacting with them.

CHAPTER 12

LEARNING HOW TO BE HATED

Having grown up running in the Pacific Northwest, I don't usually mind a little rain during a late spring or summer run. In fact, the rain can be a welcome respite from Houston's heat and humidity.

One evening, however, during a Texas-sized storm, I had Houston's largest park almost to myself. It looked like there were only three of us braving the elements around Memorial Park's three-mile loop. The rain turned to thunder and then lightning. It got so violent that a tree fell to the left of me. The rain turned horizontal, pelting me from the side. Puddles formed and seemed to swallow my shoes. This was too much, even for a Seattle boy, so I got in some unscheduled speed work and raced toward my car.

I had been praying during the whole run, and on some such occasions I can sense God teaching me as I do so. In my mind, I believe the storm provided a stark and terrifying picture of Satan's wrath toward God's work and workers. The storm was a physical embodiment of the violence, terror, and multiple attacks leveled against God's church by God's enemies.

And sometimes we best be seeking shelter from those attacks.

It was a difficult truth for me to receive God's warning that to be God's friend is to be his enemies' enemy:

"If the world hates you, know that it has hated me before it hated you. If you were of the world, the world would love you as its own; but because you are not of the world, but I chose you out of the world, therefore the world hates you. Remember the word that I said to you: 'A servant is not greater than his master.' If they persecuted me, they will also persecute you."

JOHN 15:18–20 ESV

Of course, we don't look on enemies as "enemies," in the sense that Jesus calls us to love even our enemies (Matthew 5:44). But just as God leads his followers to love even their enemies, so those whose father is Satan are led to hate even their friends—those who pray for them and care about their souls.

A couple of stunning examples:

- British journalist Christopher Hitchens coproduced a viciously critical documentary on Mother Teresa titled "Hell's Angel."
- Madame Guyon (1648–1717), whose writings brought great encouragement to such notables as François Fénelon, John Wesley, and Count Zinzendorf, was imprisoned for eight months after writing *A Short and Easy Method of Prayer*. Enemies poisoned her while she was in prison, and she suffered the effects of that poisoning for the next seven years—*for inspiring people to pray.*

The stories in Scripture and Christian history are legion—it is virtually impossible to seek first God's kingdom without being criticized, hated, and persecuted in the process. A popular colonial-era evangelist preached a famous sermon titled "Persecution: Every Christian's Lot."[1] He put the emphasis on the word *every*.[1]

Jesus was reviled, executed as a criminal, seen as a threat, and held in utter contempt—and we demand to be praised? Paul said the early apostles were cursed and called "the scum of the earth" (1 Corinthians 4:13), and yet we are sent into a tailspin if a lonely person with thirty Twitter followers attacks us?

---

1. See Mark 10:29–30 (emphasis added): "Truly I tell you," Jesus replied, "no one who has left home or brothers or sisters or mother or father or children or fields for me and the gospel will fail to receive a hundred times as much in this present age: homes, brothers, sisters, mothers, children and fields—*along with persecutions*—and in the age to come eternal life."

Making matters worse, some Christians pile on this persecution by lecturing us that the *only* reason we are persecuted by the world and the *real* reason we are hated is that we are hateful. That may, in many cases, be true. If we lack grace and mercy and speak with obnoxious self-righteousness, we shouldn't be surprised if we get punched in the nose now and then. But to suggest that if we were to love as Jesus did, the world would melt before us, drop its opposition, sing our praises, and swell our ranks is to be absolutely blind to how the perfectly loving Jesus was treated and to how many of his most noble, faithful followers have been assaulted for the past two millennia.

The reality of our loving actions, our generosity, and our service-oriented lives won't make the world stop hating us—though we should still love zealously. It never has, and it never will. The only thing that will make the world stop hating us is when we agree with the world, even when the world disagrees with Jesus.

Today's church needs to heed the warning given to Thyatira in Revelation 2:19–20. Thyatira *excelled* in love, service, and deeds: "I know your deeds, your love and faith, your service and perseverance." Yet Jesus chastises her for tolerating teaching about sexual immorality. This church excelled in love but was tolerant toward sexual sin, *and Jesus held that against her.* Love is essential, but loving acts without testifying to biblical truth is the coward's path to self-righteousness—a sneaky and misguided attempt to seemingly follow Jesus while sidestepping the world's wrath.

When we take that cowardly path, we're not truly loving others, and we're not loving Jesus. We're loving *ourselves.*

Francis de Sales calls all Christians to love but reminds us that we should not expect to be loved in return: "As the world looks upon us with an evil eye, we can never be agreeable to it . . . Charity is benevolent and kind, says St. Paul, but the world is malicious; charity thinks no evil, whereas, the world on the contrary, always thinks evil, and when it cannot condemn our actions it will accuse our intentions . . . Whatever we do, the world will wage war against us."[2]

Jeremy Taylor (seventeenth-century Anglican clergyman) agrees:

"If men will not lay aside . . . their open love to their secret sin, they may kill an apostle and yet be so ignorant as to 'think they do God good service'; they may disturb kingdoms, and break the peace of a well-ordered church, and rise up against their fathers, and be cruel to their brethren, and stir up the people to sedition; and all this with . . . a proud spirit."[3] They do this, Taylor says, because it is more agreeable to them to bring down an entire church than admit that what they are doing is sin. For them, it is easier to challenge the truth than to live by it, so they viciously attack anyone who dares to speak the truth. They live by the motto, *Agree with me, or pay the price.* This is control and murder wrapped up into one toxic campaign.

Jesus said the world hates him not because he failed to love but because "I testify that its works are evil" (John 7:7). The only man who loved everyone perfectly in every way was hated not because he *lacked love* but because he *opposed evil*.

How do we respond to those toxic people who attack us with evil glee?

Christian Attacks

Sheila Wray Gregoire is a Canadian blogger, writer, and speaker. Topically, she goes where few people have the guts to go, addressing issues in marriage that rarely enter "polite" conversation. I've seen Sheila tackle sensitive topics with God-inspired grace balanced by just the right amount of truth, only to read the vile comments that follow, all but suggesting she dig a hole, climb into it, and die.

Here's how Sheila learns to discern whether she's dealing with a toxic individual or someone she needs to listen to:

One of the biggest breakthroughs I had when dealing with criticism was the realization that not everyone was trying to engage in healthy debate. Some people were fairly critiquing what I wrote or trying to engage with it; others may use similar words and phrases, but the tone was different. They weren't trying to critique me; they were trying to derail me. The only way to satisfy them would be to simply shut up. And that I was not prepared to do.[4]

What Sheila says here fits perfectly with the theme of this book: choose service to God over submission to toxic people.

Sheila is experienced and wise enough to know that sometimes people co-opt Christian language in manipulative ways. She wrote to me, "Learning that not everyone who uses Christian language needs to be heeded was a great load off of me. Instead of obsessing as to whether or not what they said had merit, I could ask, 'Do we simply see things differently and they're concerned, or are they trying to stop my ministry altogether?' Those in the latter group, I decided, I was free to ignore."

Just because someone *sounds* like a Christian or uses Christian language doesn't mean they're offering Christian truth. Until we get this down, we'll be discouraged and confused by toxic attacks couched in Christianese.

Jesus faced this with the Pharisees. They talked with feigned respect. "'Teacher,' they said, 'we know that you are a man of integrity and that you teach the way of God in accordance with the truth'" (Matthew 22:16).

Jesus saw right through them and called them out on it. "But Jesus, *knowing their evil intent*, said, 'You hypocrites, why are you trying to trap me?'" (Matthew 22:18, emphasis added).

The language ("you are a man of integrity"; "you teach the way of God in accordance with the truth") sounded good and holy, but the motives were sinister. A dirty person can wear clean clothes, but that doesn't make the person clean underneath.

Religion, under the guise of grace, can be a powerful force for good. Absent grace, religion can corrupt. Self-righteous religion pours gasoline on the fire—"I'm only defending the faith!"—rather than bringing conviction about our own toxic actions.

If you are truly a follower of Christ, you won't just speak Christ's message; you will also employ Christ's *methods*.

Sheila had to learn this lesson:

For years I've been twisting myself into knots trying to come to terms with how some people who say all the right things about the gospel can be so hurtful and so discouraging to my ministry. Then I realized—I'm judging people too much by what they say they believe rather than how they act. Jesus said we will know his servants by their love, not by their doctrine (though doctrine is, of course, important). Too many preach Christ out of selfish ambition or vain conceit, and not out of love for the world and for God's children. In some ways, that realization caused great grief: How could our churches be filled with such instruments of discouragement? In other ways, it caused great relief. I don't need to satisfy everyone who calls themselves a Christian. I just need to draw close to Jesus so I can hear his voice about my own calling. And in the end, I'm responsible to Jesus and to those he has put in my inner circle; I'm not responsible to answer to someone else just because they call themselves a Christian.

Kevin Harney, a pastor in Monterey, California, who also travels widely with his "Organic Outreach" seminars, has plenty of experience handling Christians who present themselves as well-meaning but who come off as toxic.

One gentleman used to come up to Kevin after *every* sermon and say something along the lines of, "That was good as far as it went, but you could have added . . ." Or, "You made a good point, but I think you need to be careful you don't leave the impression that . . ."

Finally, Kevin had to tell him, "Stop!" It was so discouraging every week to hear how his sermon could have been "just a bit" better. The number of people who attend Shoreline Church in comparison to its parking lot dictates that Kevin is done preaching at 29 minutes and 59 seconds in order to clear the parking lot for the next service. He has to leave many thoughts on the cutting-room floor, and he doesn't need a church member to remind him. Besides, this weekly five-to-ten-minute critique kept Kevin from meeting visitors and earnest attenders who had genuine questions or prayer requests.

Here's how Kevin has learned to handle toxic haters in general:[5]

1. Keep my eyes on Jesus (Hebrews 12:2). Jesus was brutalized, rejected, and hated by many. In times of attack and hurt, I am inspired, taught, and empowered when my eyes are on him.
2. Keep my eyes on other great saints who have gone before me (Hebrews 12:1). Both biblical people and people from church history show us a pathway of enduring suffering and standing strong. When I remember their journey, I am strengthened.
3. Remember that suffering for the name of Jesus is an honor, strangely so (Philippians 1:29). Perspective in these moments is powerful.
4. Don't suffer needlessly (Acts 16). Sometimes Paul suffered when he did not have to. In this encounter, he chose not to play the "I am a Roman citizen" card and let himself be "severely flogged." At other times, he spoke up before being beaten and stopped it (Acts 22:22–23:11). Why allow a beating one time and not another time? I believe it was a matter of spiritual discernment. If the beating would further the work of Jesus . . . he would endure it. If the beating had no redemptive outcome, Paul was fine speaking up and stopping it before it happened.
5. If the attacking and abusive person is a Christian, exercise church discipline (Matthew 18:15–17). Sometimes the best response is to deal with the person who is toxic and attacking by calling them to maturity, repentance, and a new way of living.

Let Them Serve You

One of the "benefits" of being attacked by toxic people is that God can use them to scour our souls and perfect our motivation. The seventh-century writer John Climacus writes of three stages through which we must pass as we learn to handle toxic behavior: "The first stage of blessed patience is to accept dishonor with bitterness and anguish of soul."[6] In this stage, we hate what is happening to us; it rips us apart. We may lose some sleep, but *we accept it as necessary in our service to God*. We don't let toxic people redirect us or hinder us. It hurts us, but *it doesn't stop us*. That's the first stage.

"The intermediate stage is to be free from pain amid all such things."[7] After we get through stage one (usually from facing toxic attacks on multiple occasions), our spiritual muscles will be strengthened, and we will actually not feel the pain so intensely, or even at all. We recognize that toxic people will be toxic, and we choose to not let it bother us. We're not surprised by it, and we're not even emotionally impacted by it. This requires being free not just from toxic people's opinions but also from the opinions of others, some of whom may believe the toxic person's attacks. This stage speaks of a higher level of spiritual maturity that isn't easily gained. Sadly, the vast majority of us will get here only after we travel through multiple episodes of toxic opposition. If you're never treated viciously, it's difficult to grow in your ability to face it without losing peace, joy, and comfort.

Climacus goes on to describe stage three, which he calls "the perfect stage, if that is attainable," which he characterizes as being able "to think of dishonor as praise."[8] I appreciate that he makes stage three sound elusive, as I think most of us will more likely bounce between stages one and two. However, with a strong sense of mission, we can, indeed, see opposition as success: "When a man is just a private citizen, a sailor, a laborer on the land, the enemies of the King do not take up arms against him. But when they see him accept the King's seal, the shield, the dagger, the sword, the bow, the uniform of a soldier, then they gnash their teeth and do all they can to destroy him . . . War against us is proof that we are making war."[9]

Climacus summarizes all this with, "Let the first [those in the first stage] rejoice and the second be strong, but blessed be the third, for he exults in the Lord."[10]

How, then, do we learn to be hated? We learn to hate what is happening *to* us while simultaneously loving what is happening *within* us.

Take the Long View

Finally, when dealing with toxic opposition, it helps to take a long-term view. When you act courageously out of obedience, what happens next may immediately seem to make things worse, but that's not the time to evaluate whether you did the right thing. As we'll see in a later chapter, when confronted, evil still tries to take its pound of flesh.

After a very painful conversation with a person Lisa and I both deeply love—a conversation that didn't end at all how we would have wished it to—I tried to encourage Lisa by telling her that in a hundred years, this person would thank us. Even if we were wrong, they would know we said what we said out of pure love. And if we're right—as we think we are—they would say, "Thank you for not letting me take a potentially ruinous detour or dishonor Christ in this way without speaking up."

We may never be appreciated for the tough conversations we have on this earth; but in eternity, when all accept the truth and beauty and lordship of King Jesus, every person who opposed us will know our motives, our heart, and—once the blinders are removed— the wisdom of living our lives according to God's Word. They will apply grace for where we were wrong and gratitude for where we were right—even the "right" they disagreed with at the time.

This is not to say that I believe I get everything right. I'm sure I don't. There are undoubtedly Scriptures and applications I've messed up and will mess up in the future.

Every Christian should be marked by humility and grace. It's possible that in my fallen state, what I see as hatred on their part is a loving, truth-based rebuke given out of obedience to God, and I should welcome the correction.

It is not *me* who ultimately defines whether someone is toxic. *Truth* determines whether someone is toxic. It's always a possibility that the toxic person and I are *both* in the wrong, even when we disagree.

We have a responsibility to speak the truth appropriately, compassionately, and unapologetically without trying to control anyone or murder anyone's reputation, but it would be a travesty to become a toxic person while ostensibly standing up for the truth. Toxic people, by definition, don't respect the personhood of others. We must respect toxic people, even while we oppose them, or else we risk becoming one of them.

Jesus is the perfect example of those who speak the truth but don't control. If they want to walk away, let them walk away. And then *you* walk away. You don't pursue them on Facebook; you don't launch a counteroffensive of gossip at church; you don't waste one second trying to tear them down. Instead, you find the reliable people who will listen, and you invest your time there.

It's not easy learning how to be hated, but faithful Christians are going to be hated. If we don't learn this difficult lesson, our mission will suffer accordingly.

Takeaways

- Sadly, to become God's friend is to become someone else's enemy (though we don't treat anyone as such). We *will* be attacked.
- Like Sheila, we need to learn how to distinguish between healthy debate and venomous attack. The latter is marked by a spirit of control and murder.
- When someone is using Christian language, it doesn't always mean they are operating with Christian motives.
- Kevin Harney has learned to respond to toxic attacks by keeping his eyes on Jesus, being inspired by the examples of previous saints, remembering that suffering for Jesus is an honor, learning when to sidestep needless suffering, and—when appropriate—finding refuge in Christian discipline.
- John Climacus offers three benchmarks to hit when learning to handle attacks: accepting attacks with anguish, experiencing attacks without anguish, and considering dishonor as praise.
- Taking the long view helps us deal with confrontations that aren't turning out as we had hoped.
- We need to balance humility (recognizing it's always possible that we are in the wrong) with courage (not being afraid to speak up).

CHAPTER 13

SCRIPTURE'S SKELETON

In 2014, when Guantanamo Bay's very existence was still quite contentious, a navy chaplain invited me to minister at the US military compound that houses the detainees captured during al-Qaida's attacks on the United States.

One of the first things I noticed was that every soldier's name tag on their uniform was held on by Velcro. When I inquired why, I was told that the name tags needed to be removed when interacting with some of the detainees because many of them engaged in psychological warfare whenever a soldier went into their cell.

"What kind of psychological warfare?" I asked.

"Sergeant Montague, you're from Minneapolis, aren't you? We have friends there, you know. I'm sure they'd be happy to visit your family."

It was best to take off the name tags and avoid the taunting.

One building held people who were known as "splashers." These men no longer had access to conventional bomb-making materials, so they fused natural elements—saliva, feces, urine, and you can guess what else (I'm not going to say it)—mixed it all up, and threw it at a guard who entered their cell.

The verbal abuse spewing from the detainees was often relentless, grinding down soldiers' patience like a West Michigan winter that seems to never end. One female guard was chastised and disciplined when she finally shouted, "Shut *up*!" at a detainee who had been sexually taunting her and threatening her family for weeks. Her discipline reveals how seriously the leadership at Guantanamo Bay took not becoming toxic themselves in the face of toxicity. I realize some believe the very idea of detainment at Guantanamo Bay is itself toxic, but this isn't the place to debate politics. Prior to my arrival, of course, some severe mistakes had been made at Guantanamo Bay and were very publicly debated. But I saw leaders doing their best to walk forward with integrity in the shadow of some very dark characters.

Guantanamo Bay brought me face-to-face with a new kind of evil. How much hatred must you have in your heart to kill people you've never met? And then, when you're captured, to splash organic "bombs" at the people who are feeding you?

Sometimes, as Christians, we are way too naive about the reality of evil, the need to confront it, *and* the need to protect each other from it. And, again, some of you may believe the evil was marked more by detainment than resistance to it. In either case, few would deny that toxic evil exists.

And yet many try to deny it. Our society usually wants to blame everything *but* evil to explain something that has gone awry. Dallas Willard addresses the way society tries to circumvent the need to directly address the effects of evil while denying the existence of evil: "We are like farmers who diligently plant crops but cannot admit the existence of weeds and insects and can only think to pour on more fertilizer. Similarly, the only solution we know to human problems today is 'education.'"[1]

Educating an evil person without regard to evil doesn't remove the evil; it simply makes him or her more equipped to spread their evil. Christians, of all people, must learn to recognize, confront, and treat the effects of evil.

A Skeleton

An adult has 206 bones. If you remove a particularly important one, however, like the hip bone, you're going to be in a world of hurt. You couldn't walk, run, or stand, even though the other 205 bones are in perfect shape.

Or let's say you take away the seven bones that comprise our neck. Though you'd still have 199 bones left, without those seven cervical vertebrae, life's going to be tough. For our body to function at its best, it needs *all* its parts.

The same is true of Scripture.

Scripture has a helpful skeleton that offers much insight for the reality and treatment of toxic people in our lives. While it has more than this, when discussing toxic people, we can focus on three parts of this skeleton: creation, fall, and redemption. Just like in the human body, each one of these "bones" is essential; not a single one should be taken out.

In this skeleton, creation is good and holy, but then comes the fall. Christians recognize the profound and real presence of evil and sin, while also holding out hope for redemption. We don't go from creation to redemption, as if evil doesn't exist. We have to deal with evil, recognize evil, and confront evil as we wait for our ultimate redemption. Redemption has already begun (with Christ's death and resurrection), but it's not yet complete. Evil has been dealt a serious blow, but it still packs a punch.

Redemption gives us hope in the face of evil; it gives us courage to confront overwhelming evil. But it doesn't pretend that evil doesn't exist. In fact, without evil, there is no need or purpose for redemption.

So a Christian mind thinks of the world as God created it as good, but also as *radically fallen*. The hope behind redemption keeps us from despair, giving us perfect spiritual eyesight. We recognize evil rather than dismiss it, but we also don't give evil more than its due. That's because we recognize God's power to overcome evil, and we embrace the church's call to confront and resist evil.

Picturing creation (marriage, parenting, friendship, business, government, and church life) without evil is to be half-blind. God created marriage. God created parental authority. God thought up the idea of his followers gathering in churches. Through his Word, he endorses government. But evil seeks to penetrate, spoil, and destroy every creational design. A good creation (nuclear energy) can be turned to nefarious purposes (a nuclear bomb). The good institution of marriage can become a cover for evil abuse. Parental authority, though blessed by God, can become malicious and abusive, intent on harming instead of nurturing.

We must not look at anything in this world—even the institutions God has created and designed—as untouched by evil. When we talk about their maintenance and purpose as if we go straight from creation to redemption, we risk leaving people unprotected and unnoticed in the cavernous evil between creation and redemption.

It is a horrific thing for a man or woman to finally admit that they married an evil, toxic person. Think about it for just a second, and you can imagine how much of a nightmare that must be. What they've been living through may begin to make some sense when they finally apply the correct label, but the admission alone demands some severe remedies almost too awful to contemplate. Such brothers or sisters in Christ need the church's support more than ever, yet they often feel this support pulling away, as if evil doesn't exist or matter. "Try harder and pray more, and your marriage will get better."

In the same way, it can take years for an adult to finally admit that their mom's or dad's obsessive "concern" may be evidence of controlling toxicity rather than genuine care. Who wants to think they need to escape their parents, when any healthy person dreams of having wonderful, nurturing, and godly parents?

Nobody wants to admit that they have a pact of any kind with a toxic person. As teachers and friends, our job is to sometimes help people understand not only God's creation (and thus the need to respect proper authority, even when it's difficult to do so) but also the effects of the fall (and thus the need to break from toxic people). If we speak only of "authority" *without* recognizing how it has been marred by the fall, we risk enabling evil rather than confronting it.

Ignoring toxic people is to ignore evil. It's to pretend that the fall never happened. It's to cooperate with evil and even protect evil rather than confront it.

The Closest We Come to Evil

The other reason it's so important to remember that evil exists isn't just so that we're protected from the evil displayed by *others*; we need to be wary of the evil within *us*. We live in a fallen world, and we live with fallen desires. If I forget evil, I won't be on the lookout for my own laziness but will instead find some noble way to characterize it. I'll defend dangerous desires with self-lectures on "freedom in Christ," or I'll see my controlling behavior as "well-intentioned."

A good friend of mine is married to a beautiful woman. He noticed one time that a customer in a checkout lane was mentally undressing her with a brazen stare. They talked about it on the way home, and she confessed, "It happens all the time. And yes, it feels like rape. It *is* a violation. I can feel it." Sometimes she can feel it even when the guy is behind her. When a guy makes a woman feel like that so he can have a tiny twinge of pleasure, that's evil unleashed.

And every guy on this planet is capable of doing that.

It is evil to forget we can act in an evil manner.

We're not just created. We're not just fallen. As Christians, we are to live in *redemption*. We recognize our bent desires, but as we surrender to new life in Christ and the indwelling presence of the Holy Spirit, we learn to fight against our bent desires rather than give in to them.

But just like someone who has been diagnosed with and then successfully treated for skin cancer, we need to stay alert for any signs that the disease we've been saved from is coming back. It's difficult to admit we're acting with evil motives, but there's something about the way the Holy Spirit convicts us that allows such disclosure to feel like the purest, most definitive awakening of love a soul can ever know.

I'll never understand how God does what he does, but trust me on this one: being made aware of your own evil while simultaneously being washed and forgiven of it feels like an amazing celestial hug. We are so blessed to serve a God who makes it clear that he understands his children and wants to heal us, not condemn us.

Evil Takes Its Toll

One of the most horrific decisions any United States president ever had to make was Harry Truman's decision to use an atomic bomb on Japan. It's sickening to see the pictures and hear the stories of misery unleashed on Hiroshima and Nagasaki. I've ministered in Japan. I love that nation and its people, and what they endured is abominable.

Others would agree but add that Japan attacked the United States first and point out that every credible historical account documents Japan's fevered determination to keep fighting the war to the very end. As horrific as it was that so many hundreds of thousands died a gruesome death in the bombings, far more Japanese (not to mention American and Allied soldiers), they say, would almost certainly have died in a protracted war. *School-aged children* had been trained to fight to the death once their parents died.

President Truman faced a terrible choice. I can't argue with anyone who says it was so terrible it couldn't have been just. How can you look at a part of humanity all but vaporized and not shudder with reprehensible disdain? But it's simplistic to suggest, without equivocation, "That was wrong," while denying the inevitable result of *not* doing it. There likely would have been more war, perhaps even more casualties, more cruelty, and almost certainly more deaths (including the deaths of children).

Here's what it comes down to: *evil takes its pound of flesh.*[1] You cannot confront evil without seeing evil take a swipe when it is pushed out the door. That's the world we live in. God spared the baby Jesus by telling Joseph to leave Bethlehem and escape to Egypt, because Herod was determined to kill the young infant. We all know what happened next. Herod ordered every infant boy in Bethlehem killed. God wasn't surprised by this; he knew that Jesus' birth and the Magi's arrival would stoke Herod's fears. Yet Jesus' birth was, of course, necessary.

---

1. I'm not calling Japan evil. I'm describing the systemic and spiritual evil that existed during the entire conflict.

Jesus' death and resurrection has saved, one would hope, billions. But his birth resulted in the death of numerous children in "the slaughter of the innocents," brought about by Herod's decree (Matthew 2:16). Herod was very paranoid during this period, and it's a telling picture: Jesus came to destroy death, but death was determined to exact a few casualties before being vanquished.

We have to remember that when we're dealing with toxic people, there are sometimes no options in which no one gets hurt.

The older I get, the more I hate war. I despise it. I wish every world leader would be desperate to search out every option short of war before committing a single soldier to battle. But to say war is never necessary or has never been necessary is to discount the sad reality that there are some evils that only war has stopped—Nazism, the Khmer Rouge, ethnic cleansing in Bosnia, and the like. This is not to deny that many wars have been stupid, evil, unnecessary, and even demonic. It's simply to admit that some wars, as heinous as they may have been, were perhaps necessary to stop an even greater evil.

What this teaches us is that confronting evil isn't tidy. You can't fight evil and say, "So, no one's feelings were hurt, and everyone comes out happy; let's all hug and make up."

But that's what we hope for when we try to confront toxic people, isn't it? And if the toxic person gets upset and the relationship turns messy, we think somehow that the Christian failed. We won't think that, of course, if we remember Scripture's skeleton: creation, *fall*, and redemption. Unfortunately, living in redemption *doesn't* mean no one gets hurt.

Shrewd in the Face of Evil

Both Jesus and Paul commend a combination of wisdom and innocence when dealing with evil.

> JESUS: "I am sending you out like sheep among wolves. Therefore be as shrewd as snakes and as innocent as doves. Be on your guard" (Matthew 10:16–17).

PAUL: "Keep away from them. For such people are not serving our Lord Christ, but their own appetites. By smooth talk and flattery they deceive the minds of naive people" (Romans 16:17–18).

We don't roll over and pretend evil doesn't exist. We have to learn how to address it—always with the hope of redemption, but never with the defenselessness of naïveté. In his commentary on *Romans*, N. T. Wright explains:

> Shrewdness without innocence becomes serpentine; innocence without shrewdness becomes naïveté. The laudable desire to think well of everyone needs to be tempered with the recognition that some are indeed out for their own ends and are merely giving the appearance of friendliness and piety by their skill at smooth talking. Unless this is spotted early on and confronted, trouble is stored up for later, as an untreated sore is allowed to fester.[2]

Every war is caused by evil, but not every war is evil. Every divorce is caused by sin, but not every divorce is sinful. Sin is behind every act of a child being removed from its parents, but it is not always sinful to remove a child from abusive parents.

Understanding, admitting, and living in the reality of this tension is essential to understand where we're forced to go in future chapters. Evil is awful. Toxicity is terrible. And many times, it is a dirty business to interact with toxic people. The notion that we can go from creation to redemption while skipping over evil or not being harmed by evil isn't just naive; it's unbiblical. *We hurt the people being hurt if we can't call evil evil or toxicity toxic.*

The Only Absolute Authority

The Bible clearly upholds authority as essential to human well-being, but the only absolute authority is God's. Though we are called to obey the government (Romans 13:1), there are clear teachings about when it's necessary to disobey the government (Exodus 1:15–17; Acts 5:29). At least historically, Paul seems to suggest there is some kind of "authority" in marriage: "Wives, submit yourselves to your husbands, as is fitting in the Lord," but then he hastens to add, "Husbands, love your wives and do not be harsh with them" (Colossians 3:18–19). He tells children to obey their parents: "Children, obey your parents in everything, for this pleases the Lord," and then he immediately counters with, "Fathers, do not embitter your children, or they will become discouraged" (Colossians 3:20–21).

Jonathan Leeman makes a helpful distinction when he writes, "Broadly speaking, two basic kinds of government show up in the Bible: those who knew they were *under* God and those who thought they *were* God or were equal to God. The first kind protected God's people. The second kind attacked them. The first knew they were servants (Rom. 13). The second didn't, and so acted like divine imposters and beasts (Ps. 2; Rev. 13; 17:1–6)."[3]

What does this tell us? Authority matters to God, but human authority is always vulnerable to being abused and perverted. Paul never forgets that what God creates as good can be used for bad. If a father uses his authority to beat a child or starve a child, that authority can be revoked. Government should be obeyed, but if the government tells us to dishonor God, we no longer recognize its authority. The marriage covenant is binding and should be respected, but when one partner turns every hour into a toxic stew, squelching the life and service out of the other, just like we should remove the child from the home or the citizen from the state, we can remove the spouse from the marriage.

The Bible says these are good institutions, but when they are used for evil, the Christian stands with God—the *only* absolute authority. *We respect authority but resist evil.* This is a world where good things can go bad. When read in context, the Bible clearly doesn't shy away from making provision in such situations.

Have you ever noticed how evil has a tendency to recruit others in its destruction? Evil doesn't just want to hurt; it wants to *corrupt*, which is why it's so pernicious to leave someone in a toxic situation.

Paul McCartney was the last of the Beatles to try heroin. He had resisted the drug for a long time in the face of unrelenting pressure from his bandmates and others. George Harrison admitted, "[Paul] felt very left out, and we were all slightly cruel to him . . . 'We're taking it and you're not.'"[4]

One of Paul's biographers describes a harrowing scene: "Richard Lester recalls watching 'an absolutely chilling exercise in controlled evil' as two of the most beautiful young women he'd ever seen deployed all their charms to try to get Paul to try heroin."[5]

I wish you could read the emails I've received telling me what some wives have done to try to save their marriages. They have compromised ethically in ways they are now ashamed of, doing all they possibly could to placate a toxic man in order to avoid divorce. Asking a Christian to not act like a Christian is the height of evil. Looking back, these wives regret staying and compromising more than leaving and divorcing because they have experienced firsthand how evil always seeks to *corrupt*.

People say they hate "pushy Christians" who try to "save" others, but proselytizing goes both ways. Whether it's through seductive pleasure, substance abuse, prejudice, hatred, lust, or greed, evil is an earnest, wicked, and sometimes unrelenting recruiter. We need to take a solid stand against evil and support those who are being assaulted by evil. We must not pretend that evil doesn't exist.

Looking back, while I'm grateful we talked so much to our children about Jesus, I wish we had talked a little more about the reality of evil. Evil is an uncomfortable subject, but if we don't talk about it, evil is free to wage war against us under the cover of darkness.

As people saved by grace; as a community that lives with the security of our hope in the grace, kindness, and forgiveness of God; as a people who know in the end that God will set everything right, we must be willing to look evil in the face and protect each other from its assault. It's from the skeleton of Scripture—creation, fall, and redemption—that we'll look at what happens in (and how to respond to) toxic marriages and families.

Takeaways

- We cannot afford to be naive about the reality of evil in this world.
- Though the overall skeleton of Scripture is larger, dealing with toxic people requires us to emphasize creation, fall, and redemption.
- One of the worst things about forgetting the reality of evil is when we forget our own personal temptation to do evil.
- Evil takes its toll. When confronting toxic behavior or people, there may be no options where no one gets hurt.
- Jesus and Paul both tell us to be shrewd about the reality of evil.
- God has set up many forms of authority, but the only absolute authority is his. We respect authority but resist evil when the authority becomes corrupted or abused.
- Evil is a proselytizer. It seeks to enlist others in spreading its toxicity.

CHAPTER 14

A NEW ALLEGIANCE

One of the most heartbreaking aspects of kingdom work is experienced when our dearest loved ones either don't share our faith or actively oppose it.

Real life dictates that family ties can keep various toxic people close to a certain degree, but kingdom life means we don't have to let them get the final say. Jesus puts allegiance to *his* blood above allegiance to *familial* blood.

> "Do not suppose that I have come to bring peace to the earth.
> I did not come to bring peace, but a sword. For I have come to turn
>
> > "'a man against his father,
> > > a daughter against her mother,
> > a daughter-in-law against her mother-in-law—
> > > a man's enemies will be the members of his own
> > > > household.'
>
> > "Anyone who loves their father or mother more than me is not worthy of me; anyone who loves their son or daughter more than me is not worthy of me. Whoever does not take up their cross and follow me is not worthy of me. Whoever finds their life will lose it, and whoever loses their life for my sake will find it."
>
> MATTHEW 10:34–39

Perhaps the most poignant picture of Jesus choosing faith over family was when he hung on the cross and told John, his disciple, rather than James, his half brother, to take care of Mary. Roman Catholics believe that James was Jesus' cousin instead of half brother, but the principle is still the same: Jesus chooses the faithful disciple over the nearest blood relative to take care of his mother. John 7:5 paints James as an unbeliever during Jesus' lifetime, something that changed radically when Jesus visited James following the resurrection (1 Corinthians 15:7). Jude, another half brother (or cousin), also became a believer and wrote a letter in the New Testament that bears his name. So there were at least two male near relatives that Jesus could have charged to care for his widowed mother. Instead, Jesus chose a man of faith over a blood relative.

When we give family ties ultimate fealty, we enter into idolatry. Before any woman is a wife she is God's daughter with a serious call on her life. Before you are your parents' child, you are God's enlisted worker: "Another of the disciples said to him, 'Lord, let me first go and bury my father.' And Jesus said to him, 'Follow me, and leave the dead to bury their own dead'" (Matthew 8:21–22 ESV).

We live in an era in the church where family loyalty is sometimes presented as the highest loyalty, but that doesn't square with either Jesus' teaching or practice: "If anyone comes to me and does not hate father and mother, wife and children, brothers and sisters—yes, even their own life—such a person cannot be my disciple. And whoever does not carry their cross and follow me cannot be my disciple" (Luke 14:26–27).

The word *hate* here is a *comparison* word. It doesn't mean you emotionally hate (bear ill will toward) your relatives. It means that in comparison to your loyalty to Jesus, someone watching you would see that there's not even a contest. Your love for Jesus and commitment to his work are so strong that no one, not even your closest relative, can pull you away from your true allegiance. You're going to go with Jesus every time.

When Jesus was out ministering, he didn't allow family drama to distract him. On one occasion, he is interrupted by a family visit and seems almost harsh in his indifference. It's not that Jesus is apathetic toward his family; it's that he is passionate about his mission:

While Jesus was still talking to the crowd, his mother and brothers stood outside, wanting to speak to him. Someone told him, "Your mother and brothers are standing outside, wanting to speak to you."

He replied to him, "Who is my mother, and who are my brothers?" Pointing to his disciples, he said, "Here are my mother and my brothers. For whoever does the will of my Father in heaven is my brother and sister and mother."

MATTHEW 12:46–50

Another way of looking at this is that Jesus valued spending time with the "reliable people"—his followers, eager disciples, and earnest listeners—over blood relatives, some of whom (prior to the resurrection) seemed to have doubts. And who knows? Perhaps Jesus' willingness to walk *away* from his family while they resisted him opened the door to their walking *toward* him following the resurrection.

Jesus' example is key here because family ties are usually the platform from which we allow toxic people the biggest entrée into our lives (though, of course, while we choose a spouse, we don't choose our parents). *When you remind yourself, "I belong to God first and my family second," you're providing yourself with the clarity to determine the course of your future relationship.*

Our closest ties aren't to our blood family; they're to our *faith* family—those who do "the will of my Father in heaven." If those are the true brothers and sisters of Jesus, they must become our closest siblings as well. Sadly, however, toxic people also reside in the family of faith. We still live in the trifold skeleton of Scripture—creation, fall, redemption—where every institution, including the church, is subject to the fall.

Treat Them Like They're Healthy

Living by a new allegiance means we focus on doing what is right and stop worrying about how extended family members will respond to it. Our focus is on pleasing a holy God, not a spiritually unhealthy individual. Family decisions become much simpler when we keep our ultimate allegiance in mind. If God is my true first concern, the opinions of others become largely irrelevant.

Brian's wife, Angie, and his mother don't get along, though Angie has tried. She's a sensitive Christian who earnestly prays for her mother-in-law, but every holiday, the passive-aggressive abuse she gets from her mother-in-law takes weeks to recover from. One year she reached her limit. "I really can't even stomach the thought of spending this Christmas with your parents," she told Brian.

Brian's mom regularly preaches the "gospel of family" above all else, especially when it comes to holidays. Not showing up for Christmas would be seen as a declaration of war.

Brian asked me what he was supposed to do.

I didn't think it was that difficult to understand, though it might feel difficult to put into practice.

"Treat your mom as if she was healthy, spiritually speaking," I said. "If my son called me and said, 'Dad, I'm sorry, but for the sake of my marriage, we can't spend Christmas with you this year,' it would break my heart. But I'd reply, 'Son, you're making the right choice. Your wife comes first.' Any healthy person would tell a husband to back his wife. So treat your mom like she's healthy, explain what's going on, and invite her to respond like a healthy person would. If she doesn't, that's on *her*, not you."

Christians need to stop worrying about the unhealthy fallout of unhealthy people who are challenged by healthy decisions. We can't control the way someone responds, and their response isn't on us. We control our own efforts to be as loving, true, gentle, and kind as our God calls us to be as we live with healthy, God-ordained priorities. As biblical counselor Brad Hambrick has told me, grieving is a better use of emotional energy here than fretting or second-guessing, so keep the emphasis there. Learn how to grieve fractured relationships, and then learn how to let them go. Don't let disappointment morph into self-doubt and self-flagellation. Just because you wish something wasn't a certain way doesn't mean it's your fault that it's not.

In his book *Even in Our Darkness*, Jack Deere writes of a son who literally ran out of places to sleep because of continued and persistent toxic behavior. As a last-ditch effort, Jack allowed his son to move back in with them and travel with them, but another one of their children became so frightened by her brother's out-of-control behavior that she locked herself in the hotel bathroom.

Jack's words are heartbreaking but wise. He gave his son an ultimatum: enter rehab or leave, even if that meant living on the streets. "You're killing everybody around you. I can't save you from yourself, but I can save them from you."[1]

This is a devastating place to arrive at, but sometimes it becomes necessary with some toxic people, even some family members. *I can't save you from yourself, but I can save them from you.*

Breaking ties with a family member or having them reject us feels crushing. If you have to travel that sad road, learn to first find solace in your surest hope. You're not only losing a toxic earthly family. From heaven's perspective, you're gaining and being protected by a holy, affirming heavenly family.

Our Surest Hope

As believers who seek first God's kingdom, we have a hope and certainty that no one else can match, and that's the foundation out of which we can break with toxic family members, even when it feels like our hearts are being ripped out of our chests. The Bible is clear that to throw in our lot with God is to receive his special care and presence. Isaiah 52:12 tells us that "the LORD will go before you, the God of Israel will be your rear guard."

Psalm 28:7 promises, "The LORD is my strength and my shield; my heart trusts in him, and he helps me." When we trust in God, *he helps us.* He is a shield for us. Which means that if your children abandon you, you're not alone and you'll *never* be alone. If your parents turn on you, you have a more powerful heavenly Father who will affirm you. If a spouse goes to war against you, you have a warrior God who will defend you. These truths give us strength and courage to shield us from the despair and discouragement that come from dealing with toxic people who are on the attack.

When Robert Morgan's mom became a widow after decades of marriage, she was lonely at first and seemingly inconsolable. Gradually, however, as she put her trust in God, she told her son, "I've adjusted nicely to the single life, for I've never been so sure I'm *not* alone. The Lord and I talk together all day. When I wake up in the morning, He's waiting to greet me, and when I go to bed at night, He stays up and stands guard."[2]

She never wanted to be a widow, but it was only when she walked that path that she understood God's companionship. You may be facing the death of a relationship rather than the actual death of a person that makes you feel like a "widow," but the application is the same. There's a special intimacy that arises when you put your hope in God. God is with you, hurting with you, giving you courage, consolation, and protection. We never face a toxic attack without a staunch defender. God knows the truth, and ultimately his opinion is the only one that matters.

Idolatry of family leaves us vulnerable to the emotional and spiritual health of our *fallen* loved ones. Their acceptance or rejection, which is often capricious, malicious, and uncertain, haunts us, wounds us, and scars us. Ordering your life around worshiping and serving God *first* brings the stability of being affirmed, cared for, protected, and comforted by a perfectly consistent and unchanging heavenly Father.

Remember how Jesus' teaching in Matthew 6:33–34 *ends*: "But seek first his kingdom and his righteousness, and all these things will be given to you as well. Therefore do not worry about tomorrow, for tomorrow will worry about itself. Each day has enough trouble of its own."

Keep seeking the kingdom. Trust God to walk with you through the consequences.

Takeaways

- Jesus clearly calls us to place allegiance to him over allegiance to anyone else, including relatives.
- Since our actions are all we can control, the best way to deal with toxic relatives is to make decisions as if they were healthy and wise in their thinking. When they disagree with healthy decisions, that's on them, not on us.
- When our hearts feel broken because of tension with family members, God will surely show himself as our hope, our comforter, our defender, and our truest friend. Being rejected by others can actually foster deeper spiritual intimacy with God.

CHAPTER 15

THE MOST VICIOUS ATTACK

Nothing matters more to a true Christian than pleasing God, because the Holy Spirit within us inclines our hearts to value God's opinion more than anyone else's. We don't obey God primarily out of fear of his wrath or the desire to avoid hell; we love him and want to please him because he is the delight of our souls.

Toxic people diabolically perceive this and often use it as a weapon to wound the faithful. Because they know how much healthy Christians want to please God, in order to get their way, they try to twist our affection to manipulate us. One of their most common critiques—which itself is toxic and evil—is to question our faith: "Aren't Christians supposed to forgive? How come you're not acting like a Christian?"

They don't really care if we're acting like a Christian though. They just want us to do what they want us to do, and they're using our faith as a weapon to manipulate and control. I've seen this time and again. It's a favorite ploy for many toxic people, so let's get this out in the open.

Protecting against the 5 Percent

Austin grew up with two physically abusive parents. His dad was an alcoholic whose temper was always boiling beneath the surface, just waiting to erupt. His mother's violence was primarily verbal, but sometimes it hurt even more than physical abuse. Austin tries not to think about the abusive tirades he suffered as a boy, but sometimes he can still feel the wrath of his dad's belt against his backside. These beatings were more about his dad's anger than they were about

Austin's behavior. Beating Austin was a "release" to Austin's dad, not a discipline administered out of concern for Austin's welfare.

Despite the horror of his childhood, Austin has a refreshing, grace-based lack of bitterness, believing that God used his dysfunctional family life to move him into an early faith in Jesus. A neighbor invited Austin to a vacation Bible school one summer, and Austin jumped at the opportunity to get away from his home for a week. The "Jesus stuff" was irrelevant to the fact that he'd have a respite from a toxic atmosphere at home.

At the camp, Austin had a genuine conversion. Rather than rejoice at this turn of events, his parents sneered at him. "Let's see how religious you are when you get to high school," they taunted.

Austin admits that he pursued obedience with mixed motives. He was determined to behave not just to please God but also because he didn't want his parents to be right in their skepticism. His faith grew through high school and college, where he met a godly woman who became his wife.

As Austin reached his thirties, his parents realized they had messed up with Austin and his siblings. They felt lonely without their kids and thought the arrival of grandchildren would be a good chance to get a do-over with small children. Austin's dad still drank too much, however, and Austin hadn't seen any sign that his mother's anger and sharp tongue were fully under control, so when his parents began asking Austin and his wife if their children could spend a weekend alone with them, Austin was respectful but firm. He made it clear that he would never leave his children alone with them.

His dad challenged him. "I thought you called yourself a Christian."

"I do," Austin replied.

"Aren't Christians supposed to forgive? You haven't forgiven us, have you? If you had truly forgiven us, you'd let your kids spend the night with us."

Toxic people are masters at lecturing Christians over how they are "supposed" to behave. Even though they may have never acted like a Christian themselves, they love to hold Christians to the way *they* assume Christians are supposed to act. Their entire "Bible" has fifteen words: "Forgive as God has forgiven you, and judge not or you too will be judged."

Austin didn't take the bait. Even more wisely, he made it clear that if either of his parents tried to undercut his decision by going to his children and issuing an invitation behind his back, they'd lose the opportunity of ever seeing them, even with their parents present.

Honoring your parents doesn't mean putting your children in a situation where you're not 100 percent certain they're safe. If you think there's a 5 percent chance something could go wrong, the most loving thing you can do is guard against that 5 percent.

Austin's parents created this situation, forcing Austin to respond accordingly. He can't own their disappointment or feel sorry for their anger. If they were truly repentant, they would bless Austin's actions by saying, "You're such a good father. You're doing what good fathers do and what we wish we would have done when you were young." That attitude would demonstrate actual repentance.

When Austin's dad accused him of not acting like a Christian, he was merely continuing a lifelong pattern of hitting Austin. This hit was verbal, but it cut to the core. It was itself a toxic verbal attack.

Don't fall for the bait when someone says you're not "acting like a Christian." Seek counsel from someone who is actually following Christ.

The Ex

Diane's worst suspicions were finally confirmed when, in spite of repeated denials, her husband's infidelity was blatantly exposed. He was doing much more than "company business" on those trips away from home with his assistant, as Diane suspected all along.

As toxic people often do, Diane's ex was a master at gaslighting—making a sane victim feel like they're going crazy for stating the obvious truth. Any healthy person could see that Diane's ex was cheating on her, but Jason made her feel like an insecure idiot for drawing conclusions about what ended up to be the truth.

Diane told him she wasn't into sharing husbands, so Jason moved in with the mistress he previously denied having any romantic attraction to. And, of course, he blamed Diane for their marriage's demise. He told the children, "Your mom kicked me out. Where else am I supposed to live? Your mother doesn't trust men. She's got these crazy, insecure thoughts, and she's probably feeding your mind with lies about what I did. Nothing ever happened between me and Crystal until your mother forced me out of the house."

How Jason (a professing believer) thought that a separation gave him biblical license to immediately "start" a sexual relationship with someone else was a glaring omission that, fortunately, Diane's kids saw through. At least the older ones did.

I've witnessed enough of these affairs to know that the guilty party will often grow weary of the mistress. These guys leave solid Christian women for someone who is willing to sleep with a married man who still has young children living at home. That's the height of selfishness, and selfishness never confines itself to one aspect of character. Such a person is going to grow wearisome. Eventually the romantic infatuation will fade, and the ex will realize that the new mistress doesn't have half the character, strength, and blessings of the woman who fears God. And he will often want to go back—not out of conviction or concern for his family, but out of a selfish desire to improve his situation.

I warned Diane that this could happen. She thought I was crazy until the call came through.

"Diane, I've been thinking, maybe we acted a bit too hastily. We're both Christians. We should try to get back together. It's what God would want, don't you think?"

Diane responded, "I'm open to however God leads, but the first step has to be you moving out of Crystal's house."

"Why would I leave Crystal if you won't promise to take me back first?"

In other words, Jason only wanted to do what was right if it gave him a better option. When Diane said she wasn't interested in playing that game anymore, he shot back, "I thought Christians were supposed to forgive. You haven't forgiven me, have you? You're not acting like a Christian. How could God *not* want us to get back together?"

If you heard Jason gossiping about his wife, you might become convinced that *Diane* is the one who is sinning. Again, this is abusive talk that unleashes the worst charge you could level at a believer.

Don't fall for it.

Vicious

Toxic people are usually much better at being toxic than we are at dealing with them. They've been toxic most of their lives, are familiar with manipulating others, and enjoy conflict like a dog enjoys rolling on top of a dead squirrel.

Those of us who don't enjoy going on the attack are slow to apply the *toxic* label because it doesn't occur to us that someone could get pleasure out of making others miserable. Toxic people try to make you feel crazy; something is true, but they act like what you know to be true can't be true. The Pharisees tried to do this to Jesus. In John's gospel, Jesus asked them, "Why are you trying to kill me?" The crowd answered him with these words: "You are demon-possessed . . . Who is trying to kill you?'" (John 7:19–20).

Notice what happened here. They called God "demon-possessed." In a similar way, toxic people will call Christians "evil" when the evil people are the ones who are acting in a toxic manner. Second, they denied what Jesus knew to be true—that they wanted to kill him—trying to make him feel foolish for what he knew was correct. We all know how it ended. They *did* kill him, so obviously they *wanted* to kill him. Jesus was speaking the truth, but they made him try to look foolish for doing so.

If you know someone is doing something wrong and is making you feel like you're crazy for pointing out the truth, that's evil at work. That's the way evil operates.

On another occasion, when Jesus was calling the religious leaders out on their evil, they once again tried to turn it back on Jesus: "Aren't we right in saying that you are a Samaritan and demon-possessed?" (John 8:48).

Jesus, the pure Lamb of God, possessed by a demon! Yet notice how Jesus totally sidesteps the ridiculous charge of being "a Samaritan." He doesn't even address it: "I am not possessed by a demon; but I honor my Father and you dishonor me" (John 8:49).

He's not the issue; *they're* the issue.

Notice also how Jesus does just what we should do when interacting with toxic people: he reminds himself of his core motivation, which is to honor his heavenly Father. When a toxic person attacks us, let's think these words first: *I honor my Father in heaven above all things. Pleasing you or getting you to agree with me isn't my first goal in life.*

After explaining his motivation, Jesus puts the issue back on the toxic person, where it belongs. *This isn't about me because I'm honoring my Father; this is about you because you're dishonoring me.*

Toxic people, when called out on their hatred, control, and murder, will often try to make it about you. "Well, you're . . ." We don't have to live perfect lives to recognize imperfections. When toxic people are exposed as acting in a toxic manner—the real issue at the moment—they will try desperately to make the argument about *you*, not about them. Don't play their game. You won't win. They're better at it than you are. They've played it for a long time and with many people. You may be relatively inexperienced in interacting with their kind.

Before you receive correction, consider the source. If my wife (a devoted and mature believer), any of the four guys to whom this book is dedicated, or a pastor whom I respect pulled me aside and said, "Gary, you're compromising your faith. You're not acting like a believer is called to act in this situation," I'd listen as closely and prayerfully as I could, *assuming I was wrong*. But when someone who isn't even a believer (or who hasn't been acting like a believer for months or years) levels such a charge, it's wise to consider the source.

Think about it this way. Would you as a healthy believer ever tell someone they're not a Christian or acting like a Christian in a cavalier manner? You know that's a serious charge. Learn to see through the ruse: *they don't want you to act like a Christian as much as they want you to do what they want you to do*—and they're using Jesus as a weapon to wound you. He is not a Lord they follow and revere. Anyone who tries to use Jesus as a weapon instead of as Savior proves they don't know the first thing about following Jesus.

You Don't Have to Participate

Trying to understand crazy people simply makes you feel crazy yourself. Any responsible, objective third party would look at Austin's decision not to allow his children to spend time alone with his parents and commend him. Any pastor would tell Jason that true repentance means leaving Crystal first and building from there.

You don't have to participate in toxic people's delusion. It's futile to argue logic with an illogical person, and you won't get far debating theology with someone who is spiritually blind. Simply say, "I've made my decision. If you truly think I'm compromising my faith, I appreciate your prayers, but this is what's going to happen."

In the end, we seek wise counsel and live by Nehemiah's creed: "Remember me with favor, *my God*" (Nehemiah 13:31, emphasis added). What matters more than whether a toxic person thinks you're acting like a Christian is whether your *God* thinks you're acting like a Christian. Walk away with Jesus as he says, "I honor my Father."

Takeaways

- A serious charge frequently leveled by toxic people against Christians is, "How come you're not acting like a Christian?"
- Jesus modeled how to handle the charge of being called evil when he begins by demonstrating that his motivation is to please his heavenly Father rather than to attempt to make toxic people feel good about his words, actions, or decisions.
- Toxic people will try to make the problem about how you're reacting to their toxicity rather than their toxicity itself. Don't take the bait.
- Remember that toxic people aren't really concerned about whether you're acting like a Christian; they're just trying to use Jesus' name to get you to do what they want you to do.

CHAPTER 16

TOXIC PARENTS

The earliest biblical lesson I remember was taught by Helen Snyder, a longtime member of the First Baptist Church in Puyallup, Washington. She sat on her knees as she taught us and stressed the commandment to honor your parents. Helen used the Ephesians 6:2 version: "'Honor your father and mother'—which is the first commandment with a promise—'so that it may go well with you and that you may enjoy long life on the earth.'"

That verse with its implications was burned into me: it's the first commandment with a promise: *that it may go well with you.*

In Mark 7, Jesus excoriates the Pharisees for trying to get around this commandment by diverting to the temple the money that should have been given to their parents. It's a brutal confrontation, so I got it, even at an early age. *You take care of your parents. You honor your mother and father.*

It's easy to understand how important this commandment is, why Jesus would stress it, and why Paul would remind the early church to embrace it, even in the new covenant life. God-given authority has to be respected, or chaos begins to reign.

But as we've already discussed, only one authority is absolute— God's.

Fortunately, God placed me in a family with healthy, spiritually alive parents. Some people, however, are raised in families (as terrible as this is to write) from which they need to be saved.

G. K. Chesterton saw with the hues and shades of a successful novelist. He took strong stands—passionately so—and was not afraid to call evil evil, even when it was wearing "good" clothes. A strong proponent of family life, Chesterton once described Elizabeth Barrett's childhood as having been lived in the "house of a madman" because Edward Barrett treated his daughter Elizabeth "as part of the furniture of the house."[1] Listen to this masterful unveiling of evil masquerading as good: "The worst tyrant is not the man who rules by fear; the worst tyrant is he who rules by love and plays on it as on a harp."[2]

Notice how the desire to control others is so frequently at the root of toxic behavior.

Commenting on Chesterton's views, Alvaro de Silva, editor of *Brave New Family: G. K. Chesterton on Men and Women, Children, Sex, Divorce, Marriage and the Family*, notes that "in some traditional families, the well-intentioned claim to authority on the part of the parents may be so pervasive that instead of being home it may more closely resemble a mild concentration camp."[3]

In those cases, what God created for good, man is turning toward evil. God gives a father and mother authority to serve and love, not to sadistically order a world to their own perverted comfort and fantasy. De Silva explains, "There must be authority in a family, but the family is not merely authority or an excuse for authority, for lording over other people."[4]

When a dad "enjoys" ruling over people for his own sake, not in a spirit of service but in the spirit of a despot; when he controls his wife and kids because he can; when he doesn't see his role as service but as the one place where his enormous ego can be massaged, Scripture is the last place he should look to justify his despotism. In the name of love, he is ruling with evil, and that is truly evil, for it corrupts the meaning of love; demeans his wife, whom he is called to cherish; and confuses his children, who need to learn the meaning and practice of true love (of course, please note that a mom and wife can fall into the same toxic behavior).

If our mission is to confront evil, we must be willing to talk even about the harm done by evil parents. Doing so is excruciatingly painful, especially for the children of toxic parents. The well-known psychiatrist and author M. Scott Peck suggested, "To come to terms with evil in one's parentage is perhaps the most difficult and painful psychological task a human being can be called on to face. Most fail and so remain its victims. Those who fully succeed in developing the necessary searing vision are those who are able to name it."[5]

If we can't call toxic parents toxic, the kids of toxic parents may be left alone.

Bobby

Bobby forever changed the way my parents' generation looked at evil. M. Scott Peck wrote his bestseller *People of the Lie* in 1983. Peck's desire was to scientifically examine evil. Science doesn't usually consider evil within its purview, but Peck wanted to put evil under a microscope and examine it with a penetrating focus.

What Peck found in his counseling practice is that horrific evil can be masked in seemingly decent, hardworking, middle-class parents. Nobody who has read Peck's book will ever forget Bobby, a fifteen-year-old boy who was referred to Dr. Peck because of depression. Bobby's older brother had committed suicide, shooting himself in the head with a .22 caliber rifle. Bobby began to show signs of depression himself and was referred to the care of Dr. Peck.

When Dr. Peck asked about life at home, Bobby initially described his parents as "nice" people who drove him to his Scout meetings. He insisted his parents were "good to him" but admitted they occasionally yelled at him.

This all seemed somewhat normal until Dr. Peck asked Bobby about his Christmas gift. Bobby had wanted a tennis racket, but when asked what his parents actually got him, his reply was, "A gun."

I'll let Dr. Peck take it from here.

> "A gun?" I repeated stupidly.
> "Yes."
> "What kind of gun?" I asked slowly.
> "A twenty-two."
> "A twenty-two pistol?"
> "No, a twenty-two rifle."

There was a long moment of silence. I felt as if I had lost my bearings. I wanted to stop the interview. I wanted to go home. Finally I pushed myself to say what had to be said. "I understand that it was with a twenty-two rifle that your brother killed himself."

"Yes . . ."

"How did you feel, getting the same kind of gun that your brother had?"

"It wasn't the same kind of gun."

I began to feel better. Maybe I was just confused. "I'm sorry," I said. "I thought they were the same kind of gun."

"It wasn't the same kind of gun," Bobby replied. "It was the gun."

"The gun?"

"Yes."

"You mean, it was your brother's gun?" I wanted to go home very badly right now.

"Yes."

"You mean your parents gave you your brother's gun for Christmas, the one he shot himself with?"

"Yes."[6]

Dr. Peck realized that trying to heal Bobby in that home would be like trying to cure a person from malaria while keeping him in a tent filled with mosquitoes. Though of course they would have denied it, Bobby's parents were all but giving him permission to follow in his suicidal brother's footsteps. How does any parent gift a boy with the gun his brother used to shoot himself?

Through further discussion, Dr. Peck discovered Bobby's fondness for his aunt Helen, though (almost predictably) his mom was not fond of her sister, calling her "stuck-up."

When Dr. Peck got together with the parents, he brought up some issues of family dysfunction he had discovered with Bobby, but the dad became quite agitated. "Look, Doctor . . . I don't know what you're insinuating. You're asking all these questions like you were a policeman or something. We haven't done anything wrong. You don't have any right to take a boy from his parents, if that's what you're thinking of. We've worked hard for that boy. We've been good parents."[7]

Notice that more than the father being concerned about Bobby's safety and mental health, he was concerned about being seen as a "good dad" whose authority must be respected.

When Dr. Peck brought up the issue of the Christmas gift gun, the dad retaliated with a charge that Dr. Peck was probably "one of those antigun people." It took some deft handling and, to be honest, a couple of legal threats, but Dr. Peck finally got the parents to agree to let Bobby stay with his aunt Helen—at least for a while—and receive psychiatric care there.

Just knowing he'd be returning to Aunt Helen and not his parents' house improved Bobby's mental health enormously over the next several weeks, and the previously self-inflicted physical scars began to heal. The months of psychiatric care he received after that proved fruitful.

Bobby's story warns us that evil doesn't always come sporting a goatee and carrying a pitchfork. It doesn't always present itself with malice. It can use words of love, faith, proper authority, and even Scripture. *But evil always destroys.* Sometimes quickly, sometimes slowly, but eventually it takes its toll.

My sister is a heroic woman who has worked for child protective services from both governmental and nonprofit platforms. She is one of the most devoted mothers I know, skillfully navigating four boys into adulthood. She is passionate about parenting and wouldn't dare be cavalier about a parent's "rights" or authority. But there have been times in the court system of Tacoma, Washington, when she was nicknamed "the Terminator" for setting kids free. She has the sophistication to know how a parent should love and train a child to obey, but she also understands the utter destruction when authority is used for evil instead of good.

There are no perfect parents, so we could all be justly terrified of someone judging things we did or said and concluding, "You've lost your right to be their parent." Linda assures me that by the time cases get to her and require a judge's attention, there's no doubt that a child is endangered and being destroyed physically and emotionally.

We need the same sophistication when dealing with toxic parents—a high appreciation for authority and parental rights, but also a low tolerance for evil manipulation. The apostle Paul recognized this duality when he wrote to the Corinthians, "This is why I write these things when I am absent, that when I come I may not have to be harsh in my use of authority—the authority the Lord gave me for building you up, not for tearing you down" (2 Corinthians 13:10).

God gives parents authority to build their kids up, *not* to tear them down. It is a fearful thing to step in and challenge that authority. The only thing worse would be to shut your eyes and let a parent's authority go unchallenged as it destroys a vulnerable child.

Out with the Old, In with the New

I've seen several young women from dysfunctional homes fall into a common spiritual trap. In spite of the negative imprinting of their childhood homes, they end up making a very wise choice for marriage. As a pastor, this brings me great joy. It's a delight to see God bring two godly people together out of less than ideal backgrounds and watch a healthy family begin to form.

Then the common temptation follows. It's a clever spiritual distraction. The woman has escaped a dysfunctional family and is now settled in a functional one. It won't be too long (mere months) until she thinks she is supposed to return to the dysfunctional family and try to fix it.

My counsel to such people is that trying to fix an unfixable relationship is doomed to failure and simply robs them of the time they need to grow their functional family. Trying to fix the old family is usually a poor investment. You can't have a healthy relationship with an unhealthy mom. You can't grow a healthy relationship with an unhealthy dad. Stealing time from growing an intimate marriage and raising your children to try to repair your parents' home is a foolish thing to do. It's like skipping out from earning a paycheck at a solid, respectable company to play slot machines in Las Vegas.

I get that you want to have a positive relationship with your parents—who doesn't?—but for some people, sadly, the spiritual condition of their parents makes it impossible, leaving one of two choices: keep spending time and emotional energy trying to salvage a dysfunctional family that doesn't think it's dysfunctional and will never change, or invest your time, energy, and care into your new family; grow it deep; cement it in love; and receive God's new creation as a second chance to have the family you've always wanted.

Life is about learning to live with loss. The demand that everything be fixed and restored ignores the "fall" part of Scripture's skeleton and keeps us from seeding new life where new life is possible and even likely.

Your time, energy, and focus are limited. Don't settle for making mostly *good* investments. Try to make the *best* investment of your time every day. The closer you are to your spouse, the spiritually healthier your home will be for your future or current children. It's vital that you grow as a couple and not count on once-spoken vows to keep the marriage alive. With work and life responsibilities, it's easy to coast on commitment rather than feed your marriage. Leaving your husband and wife, even for an afternoon, to revisit a dysfunctional past is like buying a lottery ticket, "just in case." Almost any other use of that dollar would be a better use.

You are not called to be your mom's mom or your dad's dad. If they have made choices that keep them from having a healthy relationship with their children, that's not on you, and it's not something you can fix. Admit the hurt—"I really wish life wasn't this way"—and then devote all your energy to making your current family life as healthy as it can be as you invest in reliable people and healthy relationships.

The church will save untold numbers of productive, joy-filled hours if we will learn to grieve our loss (which is healthy) instead of attempt to fix toxic relationships (which rarely, if ever, proves productive). Grieving usually leads to improved spiritual health and makes things better, at least for us as individuals. Attempting to bring function to dysfunction takes up a lot of time and usually makes things worse. *When we're dealing with toxicity, grieving is almost always better than fixing.*

After you walk away and grieve, be very careful and seek wise counsel before walking back. If your faithfulness to your own family and the work of the Holy Spirit bring about a true change of heart and genuine conviction, and God calls you to nurture that development, by all means reinvest in someone who is now becoming a "reliable" person.

But not before.

Be True to Your Call

Sometimes a parent may not be a "toxic" person, but he or she can still occasionally act in toxic ways.

Jessica is a high achiever in the best sense of the phrase. She loves God and dreams big dreams about doing great service for his kingdom. She has an Ivy League degree and is starting an innovative business at a young age.

She has one sister, about five years older, who made a very poor choice in marriage and is now a chronically unemployed single mother with a young toddler. The dynamics of a struggling older sibling with an uber-successful younger sibling have created a toxic situation for years. The older sibling takes every chance she can get to put Jessica in her place.

Adding to Jessica's misery, her mother usually takes the older sibling's side. "You've *got* to help her," Jessica's mom is fond of saying. "She doesn't have the advantages you have."

Of course, Jessica's sister is sitting where she is because of *choices*, not advantages. They grew up in the same home. One took her faith seriously, and one didn't. One strove to educate herself; the other thought partying was more urgent than life preparation.

When Jessica moved back to her hometown to start her business, she started getting babysitting calls with regularity, often with less than five minutes' notice. At first she responded to the calls, but she was angry about them. Because she was the owner of her own business, she didn't have to ask anyone's permission, and her family took advantage of that.

Her mentor, Jennifer, saw this as an opportunity for Jessica to mature a little bit more. "Jessica," she said, "you've read the business bios. You know that every successful person has had to learn how to say no."

"But when I do say no, my sister says, 'I thought Christians were supposed to be kind.'"

"Your sister isn't the best judge of what Christians are supposed to do. She's using your faith against you. That's a wasted conversation. You don't have to justify yourself or even try to explain yourself. Just say, 'I'm sorry, but no.'"

"But my mom takes her side."

"Listen, Jessica, neither your mom nor your sister knows what it takes to succeed at this level. God has given you some special gifts and a special calling. What you're doing now is just as important as any Olympic athlete who is training for the next games. If your sister hasn't recruited friends to help her out, if your mom isn't willing to drop what she's doing to help out instead of playing bridge with her friends, what would your sister do then? Your niece wouldn't be wandering the neighborhood on her own. Besides, what would they do if you had stayed in Chicago? This isn't your problem; it's hers. And it's distracting you from doing what you should be doing."

When Jessica looks at this situation *relationally*, she feels torn. Her sister plays the "I thought you were supposed to model Jesus to me" card, and her mom plays the guilt card. She kept losing that game.

But Jennifer called her to focus on *mission*—Jessica is doing a good work. It takes focus, concentration, and effort to succeed. She shouldn't let her sister's poor choices put obstacles in the way of her noble choices.

It took a few conversations with Jennifer for Jessica to feel comfortable saying no, but eventually she did. She doesn't (and shouldn't) want to be selfish, but looking at her decision through the wrong lens was actually leading her to be selfish. In the long run, shortchanging her mission will hurt more people than it will help. Saying yes to avoid displeasing two people would be the selfish choice; it wouldn't be selfish to say no to her sister and mom.

And guess what? Jessica's niece hasn't been left out on the street for a single minute, and her mom hasn't disinvited her from a single holiday gathering. Her sister isn't always happy with her, but she has never been and never will be entirely happy for her. So there's really no loss, though there has been a very big gain in Jessica's professional life.

Notice the crucial difference between Jessica's story and Bobby's (above), as well as Esther's (which we'll get to in a minute): I'm not calling Jessica's mom toxic, though she occasionally acted in a way that was toxic for Jessica's mission. Jessica's mentor (correctly, in my view) didn't suggest that Jessica write off her mom and have nothing to do with her, but rather encouraged her to learn to set some boundaries. We have to learn to distinguish between a parent who occasionally acts in a toxic way—in which you can manage their assault while maintaining and growing the relationship—and parents who seem toxic to their core, from whom you simply need to get away.

The latter, unfortunately, was the case with Esther.

No More Faking Fine

Esther Fleece Allen is a millennial writer and speaker who has worked for a number of national ministries, drawing notice from CNN, *USA Today*, *Christianity Today*, and *Outreach* magazine, among other places. Because we hear of so many younger people fleeing from the church, Esther's ability to help the church understand, invite, and engage millennials is particularly strategic in building the kingdom of God.

Her life is a story of God's gracious mercy in calling a woman out of a dysfunctional childhood. Her dad and mom both had "issues" (we'll leave it at that), and one of her survival tactics as a young girl was writing a journal in which she poured out her frustrations and questions and wrestled with the challenge of trying to make sense out of living in a dysfunctional home.

Her worst courtroom experience happened when Esther was just ten years old. Her parents were divorcing and fighting over custody of Esther. It was awful. As Esther puts it, the last thing a young girl from an abusive home wants to do is answer questions about her abusive home in front of strangers. It felt violating in every way. Shame and fear enveloped her in the courtroom, amplified by the hostility sizzling between her parents.

At one point during the trial, Esther's father's lawyer wanted to enter an "exhibit." He held up a clear plastic bag that held Esther's journal.

Esther was flabbergasted, not just that they had found it, but that a stranger had read it and now wanted to read parts of it out loud to strangers to prove how awful Esther's mom was.

Esther collapsed on the spot, weeping uncontrollably. Enough is enough! She found herself promising, *I will never write another word again*. That journal had been her refuge. To see it turned into a weapon in a family war felt like the height of sacrilege.

The judge told Esther in front of everyone to "suck it up" and just answer yes or no.

It is horrific that any young girl would be put in such a situation, but that's the family Esther grew up in and that's what their dysfunction put her through.

A couple of years later, the court found that Esther's dad wasn't stable enough to raise her and awarded custody to her mom. A few years after that, Esther's mom abandoned her. Fortunately a solid Christian family took Esther in. There was no way they were going to allow this precious girl to be shuffled around the foster care system.

Esther's faith grew, and within a decade she began receiving national attention for her work. One of the great blessings of her new life was setting up her first apartment. Growing up in threatening chaos, she felt such healing in being able to create a safe home that breathes peace, joy, and life. Esther had set it up just the way she liked it. It became the safe space where she invited friends, held Bible studies, prayed, and rested. It felt like heaven to have a secure home to return to every evening.

Toxic people don't like to let go. Toxic people can't stand the thought of someone escaping their personal pollution.

As Esther's notoriety grew, her father found out where she lived. And he decided to pay her a visit.

More than once.

The most accurate way to describe it is that he began to stalk her, making her home no longer feel like a safe place of refuge but one fraught with potential danger and unwanted contact.

How much can a woman take? To be freed from the clutches of a toxic dad, find faith, become a productive worker in God's kingdom, but then have that toxic father attempt to tear apart the safe new world she had created?

Fortunately Esther's church supported her and helped her make some wise choices, including getting a restraining order against her dad. When he violated that order, they supported her in pressing charges and sending him to jail.

It wasn't easy for Esther to do that, though it seems obviously right to an objective observer. Esther struggled with the thought, *What kind of a daughter would send her father to jail?*

The answer? A precious servant in God's kingdom who has marshaled the courage to do the right thing. It is for situations such as these that God created government.

Esther wasn't just protecting herself; she was protecting the ministry God had given her. To let her father terrorize her would be to let him rob others of God's work through her. It was admirably unselfish of her to enforce the order against her dad.

What I love about Esther's story is the boldness with which she stood up to a toxic man, refused to play his toxic games, didn't let her family's toxicity become hers (eventually reaching a place of forgiveness), and refused to allow her family's ongoing toxicity to distract her from her mission.

Her story gets even better. Remember the promise that young Esther made in the courtroom to never write again? This is what makes all of us fall in love with Jesus over and over again. He takes broken, pulverized lives and turns victims into "more than conquerors." In 2017, Esther's first book *No More Faking Fine* was published by Zondervan. It's a prophetic call to the church to recapture the power of *lament* in the process of healing.

I was privileged to be among a group of people who attended a publishing dinner at the Country Music Hall of Fame in Nashville,

Tennessee, where Esther's book launch was announced. The dinner was held in the inner ring of the museum, where the walls are covered by plaques honoring the Country Music Hall of Fame inductees.

In a brilliant move, Esther had us all look around at the plaques as she asked, "In this museum, how many songs of lament are commemorated?"

Everybody laughed.

And then she said, "And in Christian bookstores, how many books of lament do we find?"

Everyone was thoughtfully silent. Esther's is a prophetic voice that is calling the church back to the neglected but biblical and spiritually healthy practice of lament.

Her story is a powerful testimony for how God can lift us above the toxic people in our past and present and still do his ministry work through us. Nobody gets to distract us from our ministry to God—not even our parents.

Takeaways

- God and the Bible call us to honor our parents, but the same Bible tells us that only God's authority is absolute.
- Bobby's story awakened an entire generation to how "quiet evil" can do so much harm. We need a high appreciation for authority and parental rights, as well as a low tolerance for toxic manipulation.
- The example of Jesus walking away is particularly helpful for those who come from dysfunctional families and are tempted to go back and try to fix those families. It's usually a much better use of time to build a new, healthy family than try to reengineer a toxic family of origin.
- When facing toxic family situations, grieving is usually much more effective than interacting and fixing.
- A parent may not *be* toxic but may *act* toxic in one or two specific ways. That doesn't mean we should cut off the relationship; it just means we need to set boundaries.
- Esther offers an excellent example of breaking free from a toxic home environment to seek first the kingdom of God.

CHAPTER 17

TOXIC MARRIAGES

If this is the first chapter you've turned to, please stop and begin at the beginning. Since I've written so much on marriage, including how God can use even a difficult marriage to help us grow, many may wonder what I'll say here about toxic marriage relationships, but please don't take this chapter out of context. I've been laying the groundwork for the conclusions mentioned in this chapter for most of the book (and especially in "Walk Away Jesus," "Scripture's Skeleton," and "A New Allegiance"), and you will gain much more if you read those chapters before you read this chapter.

Difficult and Toxic Are Two Different Things

Marriage can be a tremendous place of healing. Ryan and Tara are self-described alcoholics and sex addicts with codependent tendencies who are trying to raise a blended family with six children. It seems like a script for a disaster movie, but God's grace has been more powerful than their problems, and the two have learned to lean on his power as they walk toward healing and restoration.

It gives me so much joy to see God take two broken and sinful people and lead them into a spiritual "promised land." A difficult marriage between two sinners need not be a death sentence; it can be a strategy for achieving wholeness and healing.

Though Ryan and Tara would both say they have at times acted in a toxic manner, through grace and repentance they live a new life and routinely lift each other up. When one feels weak, the other becomes strong. When one needs tough love, the other knows how to call the other out.

I love it when I hear such testimonies. Joy overflows.

Sadly, however, the very intimacy that makes marriage so capable of ushering in holiness makes it vulnerable to cover darkness. Because of this, friends, pastors, and family members must be wise, discerning, and judicious when we work with toxicity in marriage.

This is a particularly difficult chapter for me to write, not just for the angry blowback these thoughts have caused me, but because my bent is toward saving marriages. Lisa and I can't even count the number of couples who have told us (or emailed us) that they are still married today largely because of *Sacred Marriage*. It feels like a tremendous validation to have our own marital challenges redeemed as others learned from our struggles that there is a divine purpose behind the difficulties of marriage and that it's possible to go from the "grit your teeth and learn your lessons" of *Sacred Marriage* to the delights and joys of *Cherish*.

Even more satisfying has been the several couples who have held up a baby and said, "Our marriage was wrecked. We were on our way to a divorce. *Sacred Marriage* turned us around. This baby wouldn't have been born if you hadn't written that book."

Having said that, there is a crucial difference between a *difficult* marriage and a *toxic* marriage. A difficult marriage consists of two sinners growing out of their selfishness, spiritual immaturity, and pride to learn how to become more like Christ and commit to put the other first. This is excruciatingly hard at times, but it's a wonderful process—one we should never want to run away from. God can use the disappointment of marriage to open our eyes to our sin, lead us to repentance, and then invite us to walk into a new way of life and love.

A difficult but not toxic marriage can also exist with a non-believer. I've talked to women who have grown in their faith and love for God, even though their spouses have never been followers of Jesus. Such relationships always have a measure of disappointment, but that disappointment falls well short of toxicity.

A number of men are married to women who are selfish. Some of these guys have to double down on worshiping God because they receive so little from their wives. This is very discouraging, but it's not toxic.

A *toxic* marriage isn't just frustrating; it's also *destructive*. It's marked by unrepentant, controlling behavior from which the spouse refuses to repent. Perhaps one partner has a murderous spirit that dominates and sucks the life out of the other. Or the husband or wife loves to hate, getting a sick pleasure from tearing the other person down.

We live in a fallen world where some of the most beautiful things are turned into vehicles of ugly manipulation and abuse. Because some toxicity can reach such a high level, there are times in the name of confronting evil when it is necessary for a spouse to act like Jesus and walk away—even, perhaps, from their spouse.

Christine

Christine was in bad shape—five foot seven inches tall, yet she weighed just ninety-eight pounds. Even so, every time she lifted a potato chip to her face, her husband Rick said, "You sure you want to eat that?"

Christine wasn't sure why Rick cared what she ate. They hadn't had sex for eight years, though Christine had tried everything she could to interest him, including stripteases, bubble baths, candlelight dinners, and "everything short of standing on my head in the corner to get him to look at me." Others called them "Ken and Barbie," but Christine began to feel like the ugliest woman on the planet. Rick preferred pornography and eventually even prostitutes to a real wife. In fact, he used pornography maliciously, intentionally leaving a Victoria's Secret catalog on the tub with a bottle of baby oil next to it. He spent hours alone in the bathroom and left used condoms visible in the trash.

Believing that a "dutiful Christian wife" must endure such disrespect, Christine pressed on. They went to thirteen counselors in seven years. Christine wore herself out trying to get her marriage to work, but one fateful Christmas morning, Rick told Christine, "I don't love you anymore, and I want a divorce." To be honest, Christine felt relief. As a Christian she had tried everything she could think of to "fix" her marriage. Having it taken out of her hands felt like a giant burden had been lifted, until Rick added, "The truth is, I think you're sick, and I'm going to have you committed."

Christine replied, "Rick, it's not my head that's sick; it's my heart. You've killed me from the inside out. I'm not sick in the head; I'm worn out."

The threat of having her committed turned out to be a ploy to strike fear in Christine's heart, another marital gambit to gain a bit more control over his already beaten-down wife. Christine eventually realized she had one of two choices: be destroyed or end her marriage. She chose to file for divorce herself. She explained to Rick, "I've come to the conclusion that this isn't my problem; this is your problem."

Rick went ballistic, threw everything off the countertops, slapped Christine's glasses off her face, and put her in a choke hold.

Looking back, Christine believes she waited too long to leave but understands why she put up with what she did. "I wanted to be able to stand before Jesus and say I did everything I knew to do in order to save my marriage."

Christine finally got the courage to let go one morning when she read Psalm 116:16:

> Truly I am your servant, LORD;
> I serve you just as my mother did;
> you have freed me from my chains.

Predictably, Rick doubled down on his malice. He and Christine have two children together, but he closed every bank account, canceled every credit card, and gleefully told Christine, "You have nothing without me."

Because she hadn't earned income apart from Rick, she got so desperate she had to ask him for grocery money to feed their two daughters.

He gave her five dollars with a wicked smile.

As she walked around the neighborhood trying to gather enough hope to go home and face her daughters, a neighbor stopped her and recommended, "Christine, you may as well put that home up for sale right now. There's no way you're going to be able to keep it, and you don't want to be in a desperate situation when you try to sell a home."

Christine returned to the house and collapsed in her bedroom, facedown before God.

"Please, Lord," she prayed, "just take care of me and the girls. Don't let us lose this house."

In what seemed like a vision, Christine could picture Christ walking her into a room and comforting her with words of assurance and affirmation.

While Jesus seemed to be drawing Christine closer through this painful ordeal, her church didn't follow suit. Though some who knew the entire situation, including Rick's toxic ways, remained very supportive, Christine still got kicked out of the choir as soon as others found out she had been the one to file for a divorce.

God provided for Christine and her daughters in miraculous ways—landing an incredible job that allowed her to get home when the girls returned from school, having a kind person pay for her lawn to be mowed for eighteen months (to this day, Christine doesn't know who it was), receiving free dental work, finding bags of groceries on her doorstep.

A few years passed, and the church finally seemed open to welcoming Christine back into music ministry. She worked with a kids praise program. Her church put on a big Broadway-style play once a year, and Christine was eventually asked to direct it when the former director had to step away.

The passage of time transformed her in the minds of many from a "divorcée" to a "single mom." The latter drew compassion more than judgment, so the moms gathered together to collect $500 for a Target gift card to thank her for heading up the big show.

Christine wept.

It wasn't just the money; it was the church people saying, "You're okay. We don't judge you. We want to help you."

After the show, a mature Christian woman voiced what many wanted to say: "Christine, God has fully restored you to ministry. I see the light in your face, and it's such a blessing."

This ushered in a spring thaw, spiritually speaking. Christine was invited to teach a women's Bible study, which exploded with a rich harvest. Years later, she met a wonderful Christian man. They got married and began teaching together. Christine remembers how Rick had mocked her ministry efforts, saying no one would ever notice. Her new husband attended every class she taught for seven years straight, never missing a single one. He laughed the loudest, cried the most, and said a loud amen more frequently than anyone else.

Christine tells me that ministry with him "brings life," not just to her, but to so many others.

If mission matters as much as both Jesus and Paul suggest, the end result of Christine's actions has been a fruitful harvest. In the minds of some, she may be defined as having "broken a rule" (by getting a divorce). She was headed toward death, being spiritually murdered and assaulted on a nearly daily basis. Today she breathes life and hope and actively serves others. She never wanted to leave a husband behind, but she eventually realized she had to leave the toxicity behind, and since she was married to an unrepentant, toxic man, divorce was her only option.

A Weapon and a Gift

When divorce is used as a self-indulgent weapon—when a man or woman leaves their spouse because they've grown weary of keeping their vows or have found someone they think is better—and others are left to support the victim and clean up the mess, you learn to hate such selfish foolishness.

By contrast, in the face of unrepentant and unrelenting evil, divorce can be an effective *tool* rather than a *weapon*. Megan Cox, an abuse survivor's advocate who was herself delivered from an abusive marriage, refers to her divorce as a "gift of grace."

Because evil exists, we need to condemn the *cause* of divorce rather than the *application* of divorce. Christine was being destroyed in a toxic marriage, and her ministry outside that marriage was completely quenched. When you see her now, full of spiritual life and ministering to others, you realize how much that thirteen-year marriage had cost her *and* the kingdom.

I hate divorce in the same way I hate the ordeal of chemotherapy for those who must undergo it. What a tragedy! But if a doctor has to order that action to attack the cancer threatening someone's life, it becomes what we call "a necessary evil." If a toxic person forces a spouse to seek the protection of divorce, don't fault the person who is acting on behalf of truth; fault the toxic spouse who is using marriage to prey on a victim.

Megan Cox put it this way after she read an earlier draft of this book: "The real tragedy is what happened to lead up to a divorce. The piece of paper is simply the stamped approval of the state on a devastated marriage. The devastation was probably what is much more evil than the signed document. The pain we all went through for years (or decades) of toxicity, darkness, and abuse is what we should really be hating. Saving marriages is noble, but Jesus died to save lives. Our lives are more important than our marriages. Jesus places more of a value on life than on marriage."

I admire Christine for doing all she could to make her marriage work. Given her ex-husband's infidelity, I imagine few would say divorce wasn't a "biblical" option for her. Making her pay for exercising that option, however, by kicking her out of her church choir breaks my heart.

There is always the danger that some will claim they are married to a toxic spouse simply to get out of a frustrating marriage that isn't truly abusive or toxic. *Every true teaching gets perverted in the gap of application.* But we can't allow occasionally perverted application to blind us to the need to support and protect true servants of God who are having their personality and ministry squelched and even murdered by a genuinely toxic assault.

Jesus once said, "No one who has left home or wife or brothers or sisters or parents or children for the sake of the kingdom of God will fail to receive many times as much in this age, and in the age to come eternal life" (Luke 18:29–30).

Did you get the part where Jesus explicitly says some will be forced to forsake *even their spouse* in service to him?

They Don't Want to Repent; They Just Don't Want to Stop

The reason we must support a brother or sister in Christ who needs to break with evil is that some toxic spouses will *act* repentant if they think they will lose their spouse, but it's all for show. Their hearts aren't changed. They are experts at saying to naive pastors and fellow Christians, "I'm so sorry. I really messed up. I want to reconcile, but my spouse won't forgive me. I've cried. I've even fasted. I will do anything they ask if they will just give me another chance."

They love the word *reconcile* because they know it's a loaded theological term and it tugs at the heartstrings of any sincere believer, but when you press below the surface, you soon find out they hate the *practice* of being reconciled to God and his ways. If you don't understand spiritual depravity, you'll of course want to "rescue" the marriage.

I've heard spouses recite the above script, neglecting to mention that they've already been given a thousand chances, and the only thing they were truly fasting from was prayer. They have never truly been faithful to their spouse, but if they fear they'll lose their ability to terrorize their spouse, they play the "my spouse won't forgive me and the Bible calls us to forgive" card.

Here's what's often going on. It was only when I truly embraced Scripture's skeleton that I could identify and admit this awful evil. Some people can't bear the thought of losing the opportunity to prey on their spouse, and so they will cry, pretend to repent, and promise to change—but just long enough to keep their spouse in a place where they can continue the abuse. *They don't want to reconcile in a spirit of humble repentance; they want to preserve the platform of abuse.* They are terrified of not being able to keep hurting their spouse because they get a really sick satisfaction out of committing the abuse and their worst fear is losing the ability to keep doing it. And so they will passionately pursue the empathy of other Christians so they can maintain control.

The fact that a toxic husband or wife appears to be "a Christian in good standing" can be clever cover on their part. In their desire to perpetuate evil, "smart" toxic people know they need a disguise so they don't get found out. M. Scott Peck gives this warning:

> Since the primary motive of the evil is disguise, one of the places evil people are most likely to be found is within the church. What better way to conceal one's evil from oneself, as well as from others, than to be a deacon or some other highly visible form of Christian within our culture? . . . I do not mean to imply that the evil are anything other than a small minority among the religious or that the religious motives of most people are in any way spurious. I mean only that evil people tend to gravitate toward piety for the disguise and concealment it can offer them."[1]

Let's learn to be shrewd and wise enough to oppose evil rather than unwittingly preserve its platform.

Shells

One of my close friends, Dr. Mike Dittman, challenged me to think through this dichotomy—that God hates divorce wrongly applied *and* loves and wants to rescue people who are being destroyed in a toxic marriage—with a profound statement. "Gary," he said, "God doesn't care about shells; he cares about the people in the shells."

Mike was referring to churches, but let's apply this to marriage. Keep in mind, Mike's ministry is focused on local churches and pastors. What he meant by his statement is that if any one particular church goes "down," God is more concerned about the people who make up the church than about the organizational shell that crumbles. God can build up another church, perhaps even a healthier church, on that very same spot, where it can become a new shell for the people inside who are hurting.

Can anyone deny that this is true? Shells—ministry organizations, church buildings, nonprofits, schools—even at their best, are still shells. Some go on to glory. Some collapse into infamy. Some become agents of darkness instead of beacons of light. God isn't into shells; he's into *people*.

God instituted the Sabbath and took it so seriously in the Old Testament that when someone broke it, the penalty was *death by stoning* (see Numbers 15:32–36). Keeping the Sabbath day holy obviously mattered to God. Yet when the Sabbath was turned into something that was actually hurting people in the New Testament, Jesus pushed back: "The Sabbath was made for man, not man for the Sabbath" (Mark 2:27). God loves marriage and he loves people, but do we think he loves the people or the institutions more?

Look at the nations God has torn down and lifted up. Look at the temples he commanded to be built and allowed to be destroyed. Look at the rulers he exalted and then humbled. Look at the churches that flourished and have now disappeared. Throughout history, God has favored people over shells. Perhaps we should look at marriage the same way.

I believe God can and wants to heal and redeem every broken marriage. But individuals can and do resist God's Holy Spirit. Marriage, like a church, to a certain extent is still a shell. If a marriage shell is used to allow people to be abused and hurt, God may well take it down.

When a man preys on his wife and children, refusing to repent, essentially laughing at them, assuming they can't escape his abuse because he hasn't given them a "biblical reason" for divorce (usually described as being sexually unfaithful or abandoning them)—and then he's supported by well-meaning Christians who essentially say that the shell of marriage matters more than the woman and children inside the shell—I think we've lost the heart of God.

God cared about the Israelites more than he cared about their land, their temple, and even their freedom. He let shells crack to punish, renew, and ultimately rebuild his people.

When a woman forces a godly man into divorce, perhaps even divorcing him herself because she has a mental illness or is addicted and won't work on recovery or is cruel or just flat-out falls away from God, and we say that this man can no longer minister in a public way, we've exalted the shell over the soul of one of God's sons. When we let her destroy his ministry, as well as his kids' home, we have cooperated with murderous evil.

If we're trying to preserve a shell by turning a blind eye to people being destroyed, the weight of Scripture is against us. What Mike said to me rings true: "God doesn't care about shells; he cares about the people in the shells."

Divorce Isn't the First Question

Because of the Bible's high view of marriage, the first question to ask in the face of marital breakdown isn't, "Is it okay to get a divorce?" or "*Should* I get a divorce?" The most appropriate place to start is *safety* and then *recovery*. The question of divorce is for later. The first step is to save yourself from toxic violence or backlash. The second step is to figure out what led you into a toxic relationship to begin with. Were you fooled by a very cunning person, or was there something in you that set you up to be controlled or treated in a toxic manner? The purpose of dealing with this isn't self-condemnation or recrimination, but to prevent yourself from making the same mistake again. The third step is calling your partner to radical repentance, making sure they know that things have to change, and change *now*. Those are three major issues. The question about whether the marriage can survive can come later as repentance is tested and proven (or not).

With sincere and mission-minded hearts, some spouses married to toxic people have fallen into responding in self-toxic ways. They have sacrificed themselves, blamed themselves, and exhausted themselves as they tried to cure a loved one's toxicity. The only thing this has accomplished (unwittingly) is to keep the toxic person from recognizing his or her toxicity. Sometimes the most loving thing a spouse can do is to walk away, as Jesus did, and let the toxic person face, perhaps for the very first time, the consequences of their toxic actions.

Walking away doesn't mean you'll never walk back. It just means you won't participate in toxic activity going forward. Don't tie yourself into knots trying to figure out whether this should be a permanent walking away or a strategic walking away. That can be decided later. What *is* being permanently changed is your new commitment to not enable, tolerate, or endure toxic behavior under the cover of marriage. You're done with that.

Many ex-spouses need to be set free from their guilt and reminded that the failure of a marriage doesn't mean *they* have failed. One person can torpedo a marriage. That doesn't mean you didn't contribute. No one acts perfectly in marriage. But it does mean no one should define himself or herself by whether they were able to maintain a marriage to a toxic person. It might be the case that no one would have been able to sustain a marriage to that person without seriously endangering their own spiritual and psychological health and sanity. That's not their fault; that's the toxic person's fault.

We spoke in an earlier chapter about "the law of sowing and reaping." One such consequence of breaking this law may be that a toxic spouse will lose a healthier spouse. To be explicit and clear, if a husband or wife keeps acting out in sexually inappropriate ways, he or she needs to know they will lose you. If the abuse they heap on you is shrinking your soul, it's okay to admit you can't live with them anymore. If they insist that you lie to cover up their toxic acts, you aren't just allowed but commanded to resist them.

That's not a failure of love; it's the very application of love. Standing up to a toxic person can be messy, but a one-time explosive mess usually takes less out of you spiritually than a continual toxic poisoning that doesn't knock you out immediately but keeps you sick for years on end. I'd rather break a bone than deal with a long-term autoimmune issue. I'd rather leave a job and deal with the financial mess than have the life slowly sucked out of me by a toxic boss. And if necessary, I'd rather face the horror and trauma of a divorce than know I'll be spiritually sick for the rest of my life if I don't escape.

Please keep in mind that *the most dangerous moment for an abused spouse is when that spouse tries to break free*. Separation—and that includes even mentioning the possibility of a separation—needs to be handled with an experienced counselor who knows how to guide the person through the process. Controlling people can escalate violence if they believe they are losing control. Don't bring this up or enact this without an experienced guide to walk you through the process.

Called, Loved, and Kept

Let me end with an appeal to those whose hearts are broken over their need to leave a toxic situation. I'd rather play the pastor than the prophet here.

Jude offers comforting words for anyone faced with a difficult road ahead of them. Near the beginning of the letter that bears his name, written to a church in turmoil, he writes, "I am writing to all who have been *called* by God the Father, who *loves* you and *keeps* you safe in the care of Jesus Christ" (Jude 1 NLT, emphasis added).

Name-calling by the world can be hurtful and soul-crushing.

"You're an idiot."
"You're a loser."

I've engaged in self-name-calling that is just as destructive:

"I'm pathetic."
"I'm unlovable."

Life changed when I determined that Scripture is the only source that gets to name me. And Jude offers three brilliant names for us to feast on.

Your first name is *Called*. You may have a messy past, but God is determined to usher you into a glorious future. He can and will use you.

He's that powerful and that determined. Nothing you have done and nothing anyone else has done can keep a surrendered, obedient worshiper from their future call in Christ. If you've just committed the worst sin of your life, God still names you "Called" from this moment on. Repent, receive his forgiveness, and let him guide you toward your next step. You never graduate from Matthew 6:33 ("seek first his kingdom and his righteousness, and all these things will be given to you as well") or sin so greatly that Matthew 6:33 becomes irrelevant. It's the pathway to renewed obedience every day of your life. Your name is *Called*.

Your second name is *Loved*. God doesn't use you like a carpenter uses a hammer. You matter to him deeply. You are a son or daughter, not a mere servant. He hurts when you hurt, so much so that putting yourself in a safe place is actually an act of worship. You're removing a cause of great pain to God when you don't allow others to hurt you.

The word for *love* in the original Greek language derives from *agape*, but it's a broader image. The best way to think of it is an image of God's love "enfolding" you. You are surrounded by his love on all sides, which gives credence to the third name: you are "kept."

Kept means you are safe in the care of Jesus Christ. Your mission is not to fret over the toxic person who threatens you and has hurt you in the past. Meditate on the powerful Savior who watches over you now. Your safety doesn't depend on your ability to figure everything out, to know the future, or to finally become a wiser, stronger person; your safety depends on the perfect knowledge, grace, and power of Jesus Christ.

Jesus himself will *keep* you.

The enemy may pummel you with fears, threats, anxieties, and guilt. Fight back by reminding yourself of the three names God gives you.

"I Am Called."
"I Am Loved."
"I Am Kept."

Called, Loved, and Kept. You are safe in the service of Jesus Christ.

Takeaways

- The very intimacy of marriage that makes it so capable of ushering in holiness and happiness also makes it capable of covering darkness.
- There is a big difference between a difficult marriage and a toxic marriage. A difficult marriage can foster spiritual growth; a toxic marriage squeezes the life out of one or both partners.
- Christine's story is typical of those who have been wounded in marriage and brought close to personal destruction, and who have then discovered that divorce was the doorway to a new life and renewed service to God.
- Because evil exists, we need to condemn the *cause* of divorce rather than just the *application* of divorce.
- Some toxic people will seem to be repentant, not because they want to change, but because they want to preserve the platform of abuse.
- Throughout the Old and New Testaments, it seems clear that God doesn't care about "shells." He cares about the people in the shells. Institutions he created and ordained and that he cares about deeply aren't to be used as a cover for controlling abuse.
- Divorce isn't the first question to ask when you think you may be in a toxic marriage. Safety is the first concern. Keep short-term issues in mind, and leave long-term decisions for later.
- When facing the devastation of breaking from a toxic situation, remember that God gives us three names: Called, Loved, and Kept.

CHAPTER 18

LEAVING THE TOXICITY INSTEAD OF THE MARRIAGE

I've been writing as if toxicity is a one-sided deal—there's a toxic person and a healthy person, and if the toxic person gets too toxic, the healthy person should consider following in the footsteps of Jesus and walk away.

Anyone who searches their own heart and has any sensitivity to the Holy Spirit's conviction knows such a characterization isn't always true to life. I do believe there are toxic people in general, and sometimes we may need to walk away from such a spouse. In most instances, however, toxicity and other bad behavior are exhibited on a continuum and expressed by *both* spouses—perhaps one more than the other, but both nonetheless.

A wonderful, courageous couple named Darin and Lesli have opened up their lives for the readers of this book with a tremendous story of how God helped them walk out of the mutual toxicity they experienced the first two decades of their marriage. They both saw toxic responses in each other. But labeling your spouse as partly toxic and ignoring your own toxic behavior mean that nothing positive is ever going to happen and everything negative is going to get worse.

Darin and Lesli's tale is an inspiring story of redemption and grace. It is evidence that we don't always have to leave a marriage at the first sign of toxicity. If both partners are repentant and surrendered to God, we can leave the toxicity instead of the marriage.

At Odds

Darin and Lesli are co-owners of a small business. Working together every day and sleeping together at night create all sorts of opportunities for toxic attitudes to rise and flourish. One time, Lesli forgot to pay a bill that Darin had promised a client would be paid *right away*. When Darin heard from his client that it still hadn't been paid, he was embarrassed and upset, and he let Lesli know.

At the time, Lesli lived with a fierce sense of self-protection that made saying "I'm sorry" or "I was wrong" feel impossible. Darin's anger made things even worse, however, as it caused Lesli to shut down. She justified her lack of an apology by citing Darin's angry behavior. Instead of talking things out, she refused to apologize and just quietly paid the bill.

That satisfied the client, but not Darin. For him, there was never any closure. And if there wasn't closure, he felt as a business owner that the underlying problem wasn't solved and might continue. "Aren't you going to apologize?" he'd asked. "We can't just pay the bill and pretend nothing happened."

His forceful response moved Lesli to further silence and withdrawal. Darin ended things by saying, "You never say you're wrong. Why can't you apologize?" All this did was make Lesli feel entrenched and committed to *not* apologize—*ever*. In her mind, it wasn't about what she had done; it was about Darin's response. And she wasn't about to give in to that.

This is where self-righteousness slides marriages straight into the spiritual sewer. Both Darin and Lesli could point to unhealthy patterns in the other, which both believed justified unhealthy responses from themselves.

Pre-Play

Another unhealthy pattern had to do with sexual intimacy. On business trips with an upcoming evening at a hotel, Darin liked to engage in what he called "pre-play." When he was hoping to enjoy sexual intimacy later that evening at the hotel, he'd be friendly and affectionate throughout the day, hoping to build interest. After all, he had read that women were like "crockpots," not "microwaves." They needed time to heat up, so he did his best to be lovingly flirtatious, affectionate, and a bit verbally suggestive.

The problem is that in spite of many books that say otherwise, Lesli is more like a microwave than a crockpot. She separates work and play, and throughout the day she'd be in work mode. She's not much of a talker and never returned the suggestive banter. She wanted to wrap up business rather than slow down for a lingering touch.

That coldness made Darin shut down. He thought Lesli was putting on the brakes, so he did the same. He didn't want to let himself get too ramped up if Lesli proved not to be in the mood. At the end of the day, when the work was finished, Lesli turned on the "fun" switch in her brain and essentially said, "Here I am!"

Though Darin had hoped for sex all day long, Lesli's sudden interest actually angered him. He had felt the cold shoulder for hours and had long since shut himself off. "Are you kidding me?" he'd say.

These kinds of fairly common misunderstandings went on for nearly two decades of marriage. It was always the same cycle. Darin grew increasingly offended by Lesli's inability to communicate. He'd respond by verbally jabbing her or using sarcastic comments.

The result was a growing distance. "I lived with a low-grade frustration toward her," Darin admits.

Doubling Down on the Bad

Darin's behavior was toxic, to be sure, but Lesli responded in her own toxic way by utilizing the silent treatment. She wouldn't address real issues but would instead respond with sarcasm: "You're right. I'm the worst person in the world. I suck at being a wife."

It was a clever defense: if *everything* about her was bad, there was nothing she could do—and therefore there was nothing to work on herself.

"Our toxicity fed off each other's," Darin reflects. "Lesli couldn't admit she was ever wrong about anything. She didn't feel like she needed to change anything or address any small issues because in her mind I was so manipulative and always hurting her with my prideful lectures."

Darin could prove to any counselor that Lesli's silent treatment and refusing to apologize about anything was toxic. And Lesli could prove to any counselor that sarcasm and judgment make it difficult for a woman to respond with affection.

Thanks to God's grace, Darin and Lesli's story points to the path where a couple can learn to walk away from the *toxicity* rather than the *marriage*.

The Beautiful Implosion

Change came in the summer of 2006. Darin and Lesli's church invited me to do a seminar on *Sacred Marriage* and followed up the seminar with a book study in their community groups. That opened the door for Darin to look at his marriage and his heart in a different light, as *Sacred Marriage* focuses on how God can use even a difficult marriage to shape us spiritually.

Even more significant was the work of the Holy Spirit on Darin's heart—the way God orchestrated so many events to reveal the spiritual sickness behind Darin's frustration. The state of his marriage, issues with their children, business and church challenges—all of this began to implode.

It was a beautiful implosion because it eventually led Darin to the only solution. Darin wanted desperately to succeed—in his marriage, as a parent, in his business, as a church member—and nothing was turning out right. It wasn't, he said, "until the Holy Spirit began to reveal to me that I wasn't letting the Father love me that things began to turn. In part because of issues with my own dad, I had allowed my identity to become wrapped up in my performance. Lesli had become an idol, as had many things in my life."

Darin could repeat the gospel in his sleep, but suddenly "it became precious in ways I'd never known before. The cross became precious to me because I realized it was the only place I could go. Jesus paid a debt I could not pay. I was holding others responsible for debts that weren't even close to what Jesus paid for me."

Darin defines the gospel as "the undeserved, indescribable good news of Jesus Christ suffering, dying on a cross, and rising again to save me from the righteous wrath of God toward my sin, so that I may know and be known by him eternally. Jesus paid that debt I could never repay to know a Father's love like I've never known."

Getting right with God was a necessary prerequisite for Darin to get right with his wife. He had to receive from God before he could give to his wife, or else he'd keep demanding from his wife what he should have been seeking from God.

When Darin meditated on how much God had forgiven him, the fact that Lesli might forget to pay a bill or have a difficult time communicating paled in comparison. Darin also saw the sinful impulse behind his desire to have a better marriage. "I spent most of the first twenty of our currently twenty-eight years in marriage trying to do everything I could to get my wife to understand my needs and meet them. It's difficult even to say such an incredibly selfish sentence, but now by God's grace I know that was true."

Keep in mind that Darin and Lesli weren't casual Christians. "We were both passionate, Jesus-following believers with a growing ministry, submitted to local leadership, and serving God's purpose in the church. But we just could not see eye-to-eye on the issues in our marriage that so frustrated each of us."

For Darin, overcoming toxicity began with a new identity:

God kindly revealed to me my need to settle down and trust in the gospel for my identity, not in my performance. My anger at myself and those who let me down had sprung a root of bitterness that the Father's tender love slowly, faithfully, and surgically cut out of my life. I could point to all kinds of daddy issues, legitimate offenses, and painful failures of others that might have seemed to justify my anger, but in light of what Jesus Christ did to pay a debt that I could not repay, I could no longer hold anyone responsible for how they hurt me, especially my wife. The gospel became more precious to me than life.

God revealed that the conclusions I was drawing about Lesli were not only unkind but untrue in his estimation. Oh, the failures were easy to identify, but I wasn't seeking to live with her in an understanding way, and that hindered my prayers and my relationship with God.

My need to be right and my need to be understood stood as idolatrous sentries between me and her finding common ground. I humbled myself under his loving conviction, repented for the sin I was committing, and forgave her as best I understood and kept doing so. And I stopped looking to her for things that I needed to look to God for.

Of course, this wasn't an overnight transformation. It took months for Darin's heart and mind to be realigned. "At first it was *very* awkward to act so differently," he said, "but God taught me by his Spirit and grace. As I learned to look at Lesli in this new way, I could feel the pleasure of God every time I chose to be patient, to be tender, and to be charitable."

I love that last line: "I could feel the pleasure of God every time I chose to be patient, to be tender, and to be charitable." It's what I've tried to describe with different words for most of my ministry. When we treat our spouse based on what God deserves rather than what our spouse deserves, even if our spouse doesn't respond, there's a wonderful moment of worship. Now, of course, in some severe cases, that moment of worship can include marshaling the courage to walk away, as Jesus did. At other times, it's learning to respond to troublesome behavior with the generous grace and love of God, based on Jesus' prior love for us.

Lesli Follows

Lesli's own change of heart followed Darin's. Their impasse, she admits, was broken only when Darin changed first. And men, listen up. Darin had to change without seeing results for *nearly a year* before Lesli began to come around.

Darin explains. "I began to recognize that as I laid down my expectations of her, she was free to be who she wanted to be. It hurt for a while when she didn't appreciate or even acknowledge the change I was making. But I wasn't changing for her; *I was obeying God*, and that left her actions out of the equation. In time, Lesli finally started laughing a little more and enjoying herself."

Lesli told Darin it was like he had "swallowed a huge chill pill."

"Previously, I had been done with him, to be honest," Lesli explains. "My attitude and words were, 'You're always going to be right, and I'm always going to be wrong,' so why bother? When our pastor challenged Darin about his attitude, Darin stopped doing the things that made it difficult for me to be nice to him, but I was still suspicious. It took time for me to finally admit to myself, *Okay, look at what he's doing and how I'm responding. Maybe there is something wrong with me*. I felt I was in a safer place to consider my own faults because I knew Darin was submitting to our pastor and doing everything he could to change. I could finally see where I was in the wrong."

For Lesli, changing meant facing strongholds about intimacy and sex, including lies she believed and the way she viewed herself because of things that had happened to her in her childhood. "I no longer partnered with those lies, and I was released. I'm now in a wonderful place where I can talk to Darin without those lies getting in the way and leading me to resist him."

Darin was careful not to undercut this. "I just sat back and watched with gratefulness, encouraged her pursuit, and was careful to avoid any new expectations on her," he said. "It took me a while to change, so I knew it would be slow for her too. Honestly, that's been hard. She has made progress, but it's been slow. But the difference is that she sees the need and is responding to God's grace on her own."

By doing the hard work of facing toxicity in their own marriage, Darin and Lesli have been able to reach out to other marriages. Lesli has a renewed heart for women's ministry. In prior years, she might have been inclined to join in with wives who described how difficult and demanding husbands can be. Now she sees with slightly different eyes. "The pattern I'm seeing is that there are some legitimate strongholds that we as women can submit to without even realizing it. It's normal and expected in society and even in the church for wives to roll their eyes at their husbands, disrespect them, and assume that the husband is always 100 percent in the wrong, so the wife never has to apologize."

I've seen what Lesli is talking about. Because men's sins are so visible and often so hurtful, many wives assume their own "smaller" sins don't matter, that they get a pass until their husbands become very close to perfect. Again, this is dangerous to talk about if a wife who is being abused tries to apply this, so it's helpful to have wise counsel in this regard. In many marriages, however, wives do need to hear that God doesn't give them a pass for their toxic behavior just because their husband's toxic behavior feels "worse."

Lesli explains. "I bought into the lie," she said, "that because Darin has a strong, masculine personality he must be the manipulator and I must be the victim. God showed me that it was really more the other way around. By withholding affection, respect, and communication, *I* often played the role of the manipulator."

Same People, Different Marriage

Both Darin and Lesli waking up to their own toxicity has created a demonstrably different marriage in the past eight years. Lesli still makes business errors. She still doesn't find communication or "preplay" sexual warmup easy during business trips. But the way they deal with these differences has changed dramatically. Darin said, "Lesli is more willing to hear what I have to say and consider it, so I don't feel like I have to push my agenda so hard. What used to take months to resolve now takes weeks; what used to take weeks now takes days; what used to take days now takes hours. Everything gets resolved much, much sooner."

At a recent business event—one of the most crucial of the year for their ongoing revenue source—Lesli made a serious and public error in calculation. Instead of responding with silence, she immediately told Darin, "I'm sorry. I heard what you said, and I didn't do it and I should have. Please forgive me."

Darin and Lesli are careful that others don't assume everything is better now. Life and marriage don't work that way. "The whole bit about pre-play when traveling on business?" Lesli says. "I'm still working on that. Just as God challenged Darin's heart about his expectations for me, so God has challenged me about the tough stuff in my past that isn't easy to lay down. But now that I've communicated to Darin all that's going on, it has led him to lower his expectations."

I was thrilled to hear that they're taking my book *Cherish* with them on an upcoming vacation "to learn some new strategies to deal with these issues." Darin points out, "The fact that Lesli would even read that book or look at how she might learn to cherish me is a big deal for us."

Lesli says, "I've made small steps toward being more communicative during the day and doing little things like sending texts. The big difference is that I don't see changing as optional anymore, like I used to. I *need* to be a communicator and use my words to make clear to Darin how I feel about him and what he means to me."

I didn't tell Lesli this, but her words make me think that Darin is well on his way to feeling like a cherished husband.

God Wins

Darin wants to stress—as he should—that for him, the path out of toxic behavior was receiving his heavenly Father's love that is revealed in the gospel:

> The transition out of toxicity is personally being affected by our heavenly Father's love individually and then getting his heart for our spouse. When I receive that, God also reveals his heart for my wife to me. God didn't agree with the conclusions I was making about my wife. I always thought God agreed with me

and was on my side, and that just reinforced the toxic behavior. I was convinced Lesli was in the wrong.

Once I accepted God's words about me from Scripture, how he loves me and receives me and affirms me, I was in a whole different zip code emotionally. It took a while, but when it did take hold, it impacted more than my marriage. I stopped getting so upset with my children.

I no longer feel the anger I once felt. I no longer see any justification for expressing anger in the form of rage. Man's anger will not produce the righteous life that God requires. I thank my Father every day for setting me free from self-righteousness, pride, and the need to be understood that fueled my foolishness.

We are learning how to fall in love all over again one gracious moment at a time as God reveals to each of us how much he loves us and in turn gives us grace to love one another that way. It's not too far-fetched to say that it's difficult to recognize either of us as our former selves because of a great work that God has done.

The presence of a holy and pure God is the best antidote to a polluted and toxic marriage. Because of God's power and truth, when the environment is safe to do so, the preferred path is to leave the toxicity rather than the marriage.

Takeaways

- Toxic behavior in marriage is maintained and increased when we excuse our own toxic behavior because of our spouse's toxic behavior. Each spouse needs to own up to what they are doing, regardless of how their spouse is acting.
- Frustration is often birthed in misunderstanding. Darin's frustration with Lesli's coldness was based in part by expecting her to be a "crockpot" instead of a "microwave." Before you judge your spouse, step away from the stereotypes, and make sure you truly understand him or her.

- Responding to your spouse's toxic behavior with your own toxic behavior (i.e., responding to sarcasm with the silent treatment) only makes things worse.
- Many marital issues spring from blindness to spiritual realities, especially the grace of God. When we understand the love and affirmation of God and *live out of that reality*, we treat our spouse much differently.
- Old hurts left unhealed can infect present relationships. Lesli had to come to grips with past abuse in order to correct current frustrations when it comes to sexual intimacy. Loving your spouse in the present may require working through your past.
- When there's a marital impasse, usually one spouse has to be willing to be the change agent—and then to be patient as they wait for the other spouse to follow. For Lesli and Darin, the gap was about a year.
- When we let God convict us, we may find, as Lesli did, that the very thing we judge our spouse for (being a manipulator) is what God declares we are most guilty of doing.
- Nothing is gained by fighting the gender wars, as if all husbands are bad or all wives are withholding. We are each responsible to God individually for how we treat our spouse.
- The grace of God is the foundational truth out of which all lasting change and personal development spring.

CHAPTER 19

TOXIC CHILDREN

Shanice has two daughters, both young adults. She's a gifted teacher and active friend. That is, she's the one who gets the first call when someone else is going through a crisis in their marriage, with their own kids, or at their church.

One of her daughters, spiritually speaking, is a human wrecking ball. She makes bad choice after bad choice, waiting until things hit a crisis point and then calling Shanice to bail her out. It's always a desperate call: "If you don't help me, I'm going to be sleeping on the streets tonight."

Her daughter has learned that if there is the tiniest little buffer ("I'll be on the streets by Friday"), Shanice is willing to wait. But if it comes to being on the streets in the next twenty-four hours, Shanice usually caves, drops everything she's doing, opens her wallet, and helps her daughter "one last time."

Dealing with such emergencies has forced Shanice to renege on personal plans, cancel teaching sessions at her church, and sacrifice time with her husband in order to respond to her daughter's crises. Finally, Shanice caught on to what was happening and said, "I'm so sorry, but I can't drop everything right now."

Then her daughter (still single) got pregnant.

It's one thing to say no to your adult daughter. How do you say no to your baby granddaughter?

Shanice and her daughter started cycling through the same routine as before until Shanice felt like half her life was spent rescuing her daughter and granddaughter from ruin. As soon as her daughter "recovered," she'd leave, pay Shanice almost no attention, and then, a few months later, return in desperate straits, entangled in yet another crisis.

Many would say the motivating force that allowed Shanice's daughter to use and abuse her was *guilt*. But guilt is misplaced here. Others would say it was *concern*, but any outside observer could see that, in the end, this rescuing wasn't helping.

I'd say the force holding Shanice back and keeping her doing what deep in her soul she knew she shouldn't be was *underappreciating her own mission* before God.

Shanice has several crucial battles to fight. God has given her clear responsibilities as she "seeks first the kingdom of God"—a teaching ministry, a network of women she mentors informally and formally, a solid marriage that encourages others, not to mention one other child. By dropping everything to rescue the problem child, she sacrifices good work, even though that sacrifice isn't resulting in any perceivable change in her toxic daughter.

It'd be one thing if Shanice's sacrifice was paying off and her daughter was getting her life together. But Shanice was leaving reliable people to spend time on a supremely unreliable one who seemed to be getting *worse*.

We've got to learn which battles are ours to fight and which battles others must fight. We don't abandon our children when they become adults—of course not—but we also recognize that we can't fight their battles without sacrificing engaging in our own.

Parent, after the season of active parenting is over, you have to reset your focus. Hopefully, you've invested yourself deeply in your child's first twenty-one or twenty-two years. I am *not* giving advice for toxic children who are young and still at home. This chapter is for *adult* children who are at the appropriate age where they have to assume leadership of their own battles. What you'll discover is that you can't fight their battles without ignoring yours. And yours matter. "Seek first God's kingdom," not "first keep rescuing your irresponsible child."

Here's the happy lesson that parents who have learned this truth have discovered: When you stop fighting your adult kids' battles, you start enjoying your kids a whole lot more. You no longer define the relationship by thinking you have to fix them. Instead of constantly strategizing about how to change them, you listen to them and relate to them.

Do you ever stop praying and hoping? Of course not. How could you? But you also remember that this is *their* battle. You would take any repentant prodigal son or daughter back the moment they turn their face toward home. But that's different from chasing after an unrepentant sinner who despises your weakness and preys on you by taking advantage of it. Remember, the prodigal son's father threw his arms around his son when the son *returned*, not when he *left*. Like Jesus, the father of the prodigal son was willing to watch his prodigal walk away.

The Great Physician

One of the greatest benefits of being a believer is knowing that God fights for our kids even more than we do. The author of Hebrews writes, "Because Jesus lives forever, he has a permanent priesthood. Therefore he is able to save completely those who come to God through him, because he always lives to intercede for them" (Hebrews 7:24–25).

God isn't an uninterested *observer* in your child's life. He is the *commander-in-chief* who brings in the right defense and the right offense at just the right time to woo your child. Your stepping back isn't a lack of concern; it's a statement of faith and trust in your child's Creator. The only reason a Christian parent can step back is because of our certainty that our heavenly Father is stepping forward.

Sometimes God has to let us reach the end of our human strength before we learn this lesson. This happened to me physically after I collapsed at the end of a long, hot marathon. Because of the heat and humidity, it was a "black balloon" day, which is the organizers' way of warning people with health issues not to run and other runners to slow down considerably. I wasn't about to slow down because I had paid to fly to another state so I could run on a flat, fast course and hopefully qualify for Boston.

At mile 13, I paid dearly for my hubris and slithered through a county-wide sauna for the next two hours, barely making it across the finish line, adding almost a half hour to my previous slowest time ever. One of the finish line attendants took one look at me and led me straight to the medical tent, where someone helped me lie down and a nurse tried to find a vein to get a saline solution going into my arm. It took a while. They put my head below my feet, called a doctor for some help, and then someone said, "Oh no."

Normally, if I were to overhear a medical professional working on me say, "Oh no," I'd want to know what was going on *right away*. But I was so exhausted and so beyond myself that I entered one of the most surrendered episodes of my life. I just thought, *I've already run my race. This is theirs. There's nothing I can do to help them. Either the doctor figures this out or he doesn't. There's nothing I can do to help here. I'm just along for the ride.*

You may be in a situation with one of your children where you're feeling like you've run a hot, grueling marathon and someone says, "Oh no."

"Did you hear what your kid is up to now?"
"Has anyone told you the bad news?"
"Now the law is going to have to get involved!"

It's okay to be like me in the medical tent and trust in God the great Physician. *I'm beyond exhausted, and I've already done everything I can and perhaps more than I should have. At this point, it's up to Jesus. There's nothing else for me to add, and it doesn't even matter if I know what follows after 'Oh no.' God is going to fix this, or it's not going to get fixed.*

Remember what we learned in the chapter on Jesus living with Judas? It's not our job to stop the world or even our loved ones from any particular sin. Family relationships are multifaceted and shouldn't be reduced to one single issue. Single-issue relationships ("solve this problem"; "win this one game") are for teammates and work colleagues. For family members, keep things well-rounded. Agree where you can, and pray earnestly as God leads. But trust the great Physician to do his job in his time and in his way.

Who Gets the Attention?

Brandon has three grown children—two daughters and a son. His son is out of control, which hits Brandon deeply. He admits that wanting his son to succeed may be a bit of male pride, and he has tired himself out trying to force his son into making better choices.

His counselor has worked with Brandon for years and understands the overall family dynamics. "Brandon, you have two amazing daughters going to great places," he told him, "but you spend the majority of your time thinking about and talking to your son. In fact, I think you spend more time fretting over your son than you do affirming and relating to your two daughters *combined*. Not only do your daughters feel left out, but all this extra attention stolen from your daughters isn't even helping your son. In fact, it seems to be making things worse. Isn't it time to make a change?"

Brandon thought the counselor may be "too psychological," so he wanted a pastor's opinion. "After all, Gary," Brandon pointed out, "didn't the prodigal's dad give the prodigal half of all he earned?"

I said, "That's not the point of the parable or its purpose. Besides, even looking at it that way, the father didn't run after the prodigal when he first left, did he? He let him walk away. He let him experience the bitterness of poor choices. And during that season, the older son got his father all to himself."

Whenever you have a difficult child, the natural temptation is to pour most of your energies into saving that child as you (perhaps unwittingly) spend less time and thought on the reliable ones. This is the *exact opposite* of the biblical model we've been discussing in this book: *Don't throw away your time on toxic people; invest that time in reliable people.*

If I had a child who was off the rails, the door would always be open. I'd run to them if they walked back to me. You walk away from toxic people when they're toxic if that toxicity is destroying or harming you; if they stop being toxic, they're welcome to walk right back. In the meantime, I'm going to invest my time, energy, and prayers in the reliable children who are qualified to teach others.

Before I'm a parent, I'm a Christian. Before I'm my kids' dad, I'm my heavenly Father's son and servant. And Jesus tells me the church needs *more workers*—desperately so. "Then he said to his disciples, 'The harvest is plentiful but the workers are few. Ask the Lord of the harvest, therefore, to send out workers into his harvest field'" (Matthew 9:37–38). Whether these workers end up owning a restaurant, pastoring a church, raising their kids, serving as judges or police officers, operating on patients, or running an auto body shop, we need women and men seeking first the kingdom of God and his righteousness creatively and passionately. Such women and men need to be trained and discipled. Don't deprive the church of well-trained, reliable people in hopes that you can rescue an unreliable, stubborn, toxic relative—even a son or daughter.

If you have a reliable child who is qualified to teach others, one of the greatest gifts you can give to the church is to invest deeply in that child's mind and soul and imbue them with earnest passion to seek first the kingdom of God. *Don't make the reliable children pay for the unreliability of their sibling(s).*

Also, don't make *your own mission* for God pay for the toxic selfishness of your child. Shanice is called by God and gifted by God, and her ministry matters. Her daughter may never accomplish God's intended purpose for her life (which is truly sad), but it would be a double tragedy if Shanice let her daughter get in the way of God's will for *her* own life as well. Limit the irresponsible to their own irresponsibility. Don't let it spread to become yours.

A Tale of Two Priorities

In the parable of the ten virgins, five women forgot to bring enough oil to last through the night, while five did bring enough. The absent-minded bridesmaids saw their lamps go out at the absolute worst time and begged the responsible bridesmaids to sacrifice some of theirs. The responsible ones replied, "There may not be enough for both us and you. Instead, go to those who sell oil and buy some for yourselves" (Matthew 25:9).

You know what happened next: the irresponsible ones took too long to return and missed out on the banquet.

Jesus doesn't fault the "wise" women for refusing to sacrifice themselves; he faults the "foolish" women for the inattention that led to their crisis.

If you have an extra shirt to give to a toxic person, be kind. If you can give to a difficult individual without taking time away from a reliable individual, go for it. But if your investment of time and money keeps you from fulfilling your ministry and fighting your own battles, including investing in other reliable people, it's time to reevaluate. It's time to say no—even to your children.

The Promise No Parent Wants to Claim

Arianna was heartsick over the moral choices her son was making. Even more heartrending was his answer when Arianna asked him about where he saw Jesus in all of this.

"I'm having to rethink that," her son said. "I've had questions about him for some time."

Those may have been the most painful words Arianna had ever heard, and she launched into a self-directed diatribe about where she had gone wrong as a mother. Maybe she should have homeschooled him. Maybe she had been too busy when he was a teenager. Maybe she hadn't emphasized faith quite enough.

When kids become adults, parents face an entirely new kind of vulnerability. When our kids were young, we feared for their safety, but we could control so much of their environment that those fears could be managed. When children leave home, "control" would be evil and toxic. They are their own men and women now. And their choices may break our hearts, which is an entirely different kind of pain.

It's difficult as a pastor to break the sad news that loving Jesus with all your heart, raising your children in a solid church, and taking time at home to instill the basics of the faith *don't guarantee* any particular outcome. We're not programming computers; we're raising young women and men made in the image of God, and that image includes the ability to make choices.

I led Arianna to Mark 13:12–13, where Jesus, *talking to believers*, says, "Children will rebel against their parents and have them put to death. Everyone will hate you because of me." In a promise that none of us want to claim, Jesus foretold that some believers would see their children rebel, not just against them, but against their Lord. Our sharing in the sufferings of Christ will have to include sharing in the heartbreak of loved ones who walk away from practicing the truth.

Arianna's response was classic: "I prefer the verse about training up a child in the way he should go and in the end he won't depart from it."

We both laughed. Don't we all?

Another severe promise from Jesus seems to focus particularly on children: "From now on there will be five in one family divided against each other, three against two and two against three. They will be divided, father against son and son against father, mother against daughter and daughter against mother, mother-in-law against daughter-in-law and daughter-in-law against mother-in-law" (Luke 12:52–53).

Kingdom work is contentious. There's no getting around it. And if we so identify with kingdom work that it becomes a part of who we are (as Jesus urges us to do), when others reject that kingdom, it will likely lead to them rejecting and turning against us.

That doesn't mean you've failed. Jesus told you it would happen *not to condemn you but to prepare you.*

Dr. Steve Wilke tells grieving parents awash in guilt, "When God created the perfect world for Adam and Eve and even that wasn't enough to keep them from sinning, do you think the Trinity asked, *Where did we go wrong?*"[1]

We could also consider King David, whom God called out of nowhere and made a man of great significance, even to the point of placing him on a throne. David responded with adultery and murder. Do you think God wondered, *What could I have done differently? If only I had been a better father!*

When Jesus lived as the perfect Messiah, giving Judas wondrous teaching, perfect counsel, and absolutely the best example anyone could ever offer, and yet all that proved not to be enough for Judas, did Jesus ask, *What did I do wrong?*

Thinking we can be such good parents that our children will never stray is to think we can outdo the Trinity. You cannot as a parent create a perfect Eden experience for your kids, but even if you did, they'd mess it up.

If anything, the real answer to "what did I do wrong?" is "you were born in sin and you live in a world where every family member has been born in sin."

The heresy behind thinking you caused it is the logical extension that *you can fix it*. God's remedy for rebellion, however, isn't you; it's *Jesus*. His grace, his forgiveness, his wisdom, his power, his redemption—that's the ultimate solution, the ultimate "refuge." As much as we'd like to be, we are not the answer; Jesus is.

Jesus, by the way, is also *our hope*. When a son says, "You're not my father," that doesn't stop a loving father from saying, "But you're still my son." That's the hope for parents who see kids walk away. There's a sacrifice for their sin—Jesus' death and resurrection—a loving heavenly Father who still claims them, and a powerful Holy Spirit working overtime to convict them and bring them back.

Our children's initial salvation never depended on us—most of us know that. Here's the refuge for brokenhearted parents: their return doesn't depend on us either.

Takeaways

- Parent, your mission matters. Don't sacrifice fighting your own battles in order to try to rescue your children from the consequences of not fighting their battles.
- Because God is the great spiritual Physician, you can continue to enjoy your children without always trying to fix them, knowing that God is at work behind the scenes in ways you'll never understand.

- Don't make reliable children pay for the distraction of the un-reliable one(s). Keep your focus on investing in the reliable ones. We need more workers!
- In one of Jesus' parables, he faults the irresponsible for being unprepared; he doesn't fault the responsible for not rescuing the irresponsible.
- In a difficult teaching, Jesus warns parents that some of their children will not follow God, and that means the children may turn against their parents as well.
- Our hope must be placed in God's ability and willingness to reclaim prodigals, not in our ability to find the right things to say or do.

CHAPTER 20

TRADING TOXIC FOR TENDER

"I didn't care about people," Doug confesses. "I didn't care who I walked over and how I treated them. I might as well have been an ancient Egyptian slave master at work. I was probably worse than that, because I was as capable of walking into a meeting and cussing my boss out if I felt I wasn't getting the support I needed as I was running roughshod over the ones who were working for me. I thought you had to be like that to get anything accomplished."

Doug carried his toxic attitude into outside-of-work activities. He'd go online to an automotive forum, where he'd be intentionally abrasive and "often downright mean-spirited. It was a place where I could let loose all my anger and temper. I became one of the most knowledgeable members just so I could lord it over those less so and essentially abuse them. I go back and read some of what I said in there, and I am ashamed. It isn't like someone occasionally offended me and I reacted inappropriately. I sought out victims and was deliberate in my attacks. I was addicted to the conflict and would do everything I could to stir it up. It was a nonstop obsession for me."

Remember earlier in the book when we talked about how toxic people *enjoy* conflict? Notice Doug's language. He was "addicted to the conflict" and went out of his way to create it.

Doug makes this candid admission:

My anger permeated every relationship, from my wife and son to supervisors, peers, and subordinates, and even random people I encountered in day-to-day living. I was always ready to be angry.

Little things like a lawnmower not starting or a misplaced wrench were once massive problems for me. I looked for things to be angry about, and my anger wasn't in proportion to the severity of the offense. It was all or nothing, and usually that meant all. I look back on it now, and I don't understand why I was so consumed by it, but I think it was rooted in not being in control. It was certainly more severe when events were outside my control. A flat tire was a reason to rage. An unexpected delay or a change of plans involving work was cause to unload on my employers. Production goals not meeting my expectations drew my wrath upon my subordinates. Being cut off or otherwise offended in traffic demanded a response. An equipment breakdown, especially if I could blame someone for it, was reason enough to swear and throw tools. There was nothing that I just let go of.

Doug's behavior typifies the "loving hate" definition of toxicity from chapter 5—people who are fueled, energized, and motivated by hate. His eventual transformation is an inspiring story about how the love and grace of God can lead us away from our own toxicity. Doug's situation may sound like an extreme case, but if we truly hate toxic behavior, our vendetta must begin with the toxicity coming from *us*, wherever we fall on the spectrum.

We should especially be on the lookout for when, perhaps out of busyness, irritability, tiredness, past hurts, or spiritual sickness, we start acting in a toxic way. Franciscan priest Richard Rohr writes, "I am most quoted for this line: *'If you do not transform your pain, you will always transmit it.'* Always someone else has to suffer because I don't know how to suffer; that is what it comes down to."[1]

The only person we are called to control is ourselves. Self-control is a biblical command and a fruit of the Spirit. Trying to control others, as we've seen, is a murderous strategy from Satan. The first line of defense against toxicity in the world must therefore be launched by believers who practice *self*-control.

No discussion of toxicity would be complete without addressing Scripture's call for each of us to individually leave our own toxic ways.

Paul's words to the Colossians are particularly fascinating because he was writing to a young Christian community that didn't really know how Christians were supposed to act. They didn't have Christian grandparents who had been believers before them. They didn't know any mature believers who had spent decades walking in the faith and who could model the way Christians live. In Colossae, faith was *brand-new*. Everyone was a pioneer of sorts, with no generational influence to build on. They were the first Christians they had ever known, forcing Paul to be clear and precise as he taught them how to behave. Without getting all flowery, Paul writes to the Colossians with explicit and specific words: *This is how Christians act. This is how our faith and belief affect our attitudes and actions.*

Paul tells the Colossians that a central element of behaving like a believer is first taking something off: "But now you must also rid yourselves of all such things as these: anger, rage, malice, slander, and filthy language from your lips" (Colossians 3:8).

In other words, "Don't be toxic." The entire human disposition that intentionally hurts others has to die in us.

Paul then tells the Colossians what they are to put on: "Therefore, as God's chosen people, holy and dearly loved, clothe yourselves with compassion, kindness, humility, gentleness and patience" (Colossians 3:12). These qualities are the polar opposites of toxicity. Compassion means you feel for others rather than setting yourself against them. Kindness means you want to help, not hurt. Humility puts others first instead of wanting to control them. Gentleness means you are tender, not harsh, and patience means you are encouraging rather than abrasive.

Notice something that is crucial for personal transformation: before Paul tells the Colossians *how to behave*, he reminds them of *how much they are loved and prized by God*: "as God's chosen people, holy and dearly loved."

Knowing we are chosen and loved by God is the essential mind-set through which we love others and reject being toxic. With all our spiritual needs met in God, we can live in a toxic world without becoming toxic ourselves, provided we remember we are chosen and dearly loved. Because we live in a toxic world filled with toxic people, we *will* be treated in a toxic manner. We avoid responding in a toxic way by living out of and being motivated by the *gracious love of God*, who chose us when we were still living toxic lives and who ushers us into gracious living.

Toxic people find sick satisfaction in being mean, controlling, and hurtful. Believers find true satisfaction in being chosen and loved by God. That love is so overwhelming that we don't expect people to meet our needs. We don't want to control people or hurt people; we want people to experience the same joy and satisfaction in God that we have come to know.

God's love and affirmation lift us to a dimension of living where fighting each other doesn't make sense. When I feel spoiled by God, what you do to me or think about me doesn't matter all that much, because God's opinion is superior to yours. God's protection makes me feel secure in the face of your assault. God's affirmation speaks louder than your opposition or hatred. One of the primary ways we show that God has taken such good care of us spiritually is by how we take care of others.

Tackling His Own Toxicity

Doug's anger began to die on what he describes as his personal "Damascus road." He was sitting in a motel in Houston, Texas, promising himself "for the hundredth time" that he was done with pornography. A methodical man, Doug went online to see what others had to say about breaking porn's stranglehold, and he came across a Christian forum.

The wives' reaction to their husbands' porn use shocked Doug and helped him understand how much pain his online habits had caused his wife. He started commenting on the site, with a caveat: "I'm not a Christian. I don't want to be a Christian. In fact, I don't want anything to do with you, but you might know something I need to know about this porn stuff, so I'm looking for information on that."

Because of Doug's abrasive anger, a pastor on the forum asked Doug to stop posting publicly, but he kept communicating with Doug privately.

Doug felt moved to write what he thought would be a short apology letter to his wife, swearing off all future use of porn and asking for his wife's forgiveness. Reading of the other wives' pain somehow made Doug sensitive to *all* the ways he had failed as a husband (beyond using porn), and his "short apology letter" expanded to seven pages.

"It was the turning point in our marriage," Doug relates. "It just became clear to me how my anger was controlling me. My wife's stepfather was an angry guy. I never wanted to be that guy, but I realized I was even worse than him in some ways. Not physically, but verbally and emotionally. That realization broke me. I said to myself, *I can't be that person anymore. I don't know who I'm going to be, but I can't be that person anymore.*"

Through the pastor's private counsel and Doug's eventual attendance at a Celebrate Recovery group, Doug surrendered to the lordship of Jesus Christ. The presence of the Holy Spirit in his life, along with the lessons he learned about addiction through Celebrate Recovery, transformed every aspect of his life as he left the toxic anger and hatred behind.

"I'm slowly developing some skills that I am sorely in need of. One of the major changes in my daily life has been learning new ways to handle people when my previous techniques would have been anger, abuse, and bullying. Those habits didn't fit at work or marriage, and the new habits of listening and patience and giving up control are starting to feel almost as familiar to me as anger used to."

Christian Meanness

Unfortunately, in spite of Paul's clear and compelling words to the Colossians, today's church is not known for rejecting meanness.

In fact, many think of the church as particularly mean, especially to those who don't agree with us.

Dallas Willard was once asked why Christians are so mean. He responded by saying that Christians tend to be mean to the degree that they value being right over being like Christ. The two aren't mutually exclusive, of course, but we can make them that way when instead of receiving the words of Jesus and the writings of Paul as love letters from God to those who are chosen and loved, we use them as verbal weapons to wage war against people who don't yet believe.

I don't want you to rush by that last sentence. God's directives and "rules" in the New Testament aren't intended to be verbal grenades that we lob at people who don't believe. When someone doesn't accept Jesus' authority, we can't expect them to listen to what the Bible teaches. When God has won over our hearts, we understand that his revealed words regarding appropriate behavior are birthed in love and ultimately given for our best interests. *We won't love God's words until we first love God, so keep first things first.* Taunting people even with the truth can become toxic in a controlling sort of way. It's still taunting. Methods *matter*.

Remember, Rosaria Butterfield's friend didn't even bring up her sexual behavior; he believed, rightly, that the real issue was her alienation from God. Change for Darin came when he realized the truth of the gospel and let it penetrate his heart. Transformation for Doug occurred when he met Jesus on his personal "Damascus road."

Sermons on right living should come *after* Jesus, not before.

What should scare all of us believers a little bit is that when we listen to Jesus, he seemed to show the most compassion toward sexual sinners and more judgment toward mean people: "But I say to you that if you are angry with a brother or sister, you will be liable to judgment; and if you insult a brother or sister, you will be liable to the council; and if you say, 'You fool,' you will be liable to the hell of fire" (Matthew 5:22 NRSV).

Jesus challenges expressions of meanness because he loves the people we're being mean to. If they know him, he wants them to embrace the abundant life. If they don't know him, he wants us to display the kindness and compassion of Christ that we've received in order to invite them into his family.

When we insult others, when we call them idiots and fools, that's the kind of thing Jesus says can get us thrown into hell. If Jesus looked at your Facebook feed, if he followed your anonymous comments on other blogs, would he discern that you're demeaning anyone? In the name of serving Jesus, are you perhaps acting in a toxic manner?

God loves sinners; God wants to redeem sinners. God is in the business of taking seemingly ruined lives and turning them into beautiful, loving, and productive lives. As God's followers, we are not to mock, taunt, ridicule, or bully any "sinner." Being mean to someone we consider a sinner is itself a toxic sin. We're adding to the problem, not offering ourselves as instruments of the solution.

Instead of being toxic, we are called to show compassion.

Spiritual Meningitis

A Christian college invited me to be the guest lecturer at an endowed lecture series. The professor who introduced me crawled up the stage stairs on all fours, using his hands. There weren't many stairs, maybe six or eight, and the stage wasn't that high, but he was crawling on his way to the stage.

He didn't say anything about this, nor did anyone act like anything unusual had occurred.

To me, it just seemed bizarre.

Afterward, I found out the story behind his actions. This professor had suffered a bout with viral meningitis; he had recovered, but the meningitis had affected his balance. The stage didn't have a railing, and the only way he could get up safely was to crawl.

A wave of compassion washed over me. What humility it must take for an esteemed professor to confront such physical limitations in such a public setting, where everyone would see and many like me would not know what's going on.

I felt a little like I had watched a modern-day Francis of Assisi in action, who had purposely worn what was then considered children's clothing as an act of personal humility. Anyone who knows this professor's story would feel similar compassion. Ridicule would be the last thing that came to mind.

This is one of the keys to not becoming toxic on our own. Can you feel compassion when evil has invaded your coworker or family member and left deleterious results? Instead of feeling put out by their weakness, can you feel empathy?

Of course, there are consequences and boundaries. For example, no mother or father would let this professor carry their baby up those steps! But if they knew his backstory, they would find a nontoxic way to tell him why.

Pretty much every sinner has a backstory. This isn't to excuse how they've responded or what they've done. But remembering there's a backstory can help us maintain that all-important compassion so that we ourselves don't become toxic in the face of others' toxicity.

When people become flooded with fear and insecurity and they've been surrounded by toxic behavior from childhood, they are susceptible to becoming toxic themselves. If you've been sick for a long time, you are far more likely to display impatience. If you are lonely and shamed, you are far more susceptible to gluttony or lust. That doesn't excuse you, but it explains what often sets you up, and this fallen world is adept at setting us up for toxic behavior.

All this is simply to call us to *compassion first*. Compassion doesn't mean you allow hurt people to keep hurting you. But it does mean you grieve for the hurt that leads them to hurt others. Mixed in with your anger is sorrow that someone chose the wrong path in a misguided attempt at self-defense.

Unless you are in a position of authority where it is your responsibility to protect others, you don't have to punish toxic people on your own; leave that to God. One of the things that helps me is remembering that *a toxic person's life is its own punishment*. It must be misery indeed to be filled with hate, division, malice, rage, and murder, wanting to control people instead of loving and encouraging them. Toxic people must always live on the precipice of fear and exposure. They are terrified by the light and the truth, yet the light and the truth will win out in the end.

If we think about it, we would all (hopefully) rather be accused by them and accepted by God than be accepted by them and rejected by God. They're playing for the losing team.

In opposing them, however, let's consciously avoid becoming like them.

But let's also remember that the goal of life isn't *not* being toxic; the goal of life is the compassion, kindness, humility, gentleness, and patience that come from knowing we are chosen and dearly loved by God.

Everything Must Change

When Doug finally left his toxic behavior behind, he had to learn how to work and be married all over again. Everything was different. "The honest truth is that I just didn't know how to do my job without my anger, and I really struggled because of it. I even wondered if I would ever be able to succeed. Instead of being angry and lashing out when others let me down, I had to find another way, and that took time."

Gaining control of his toxic behavior has had a lot of applications for Doug. Rather recently, his wife had serious surgery. In the past, Doug's worst behavior showed up when he couldn't control what was happening. During one of her previous surgeries, for example, Doug confesses, "I was beside myself with anxiety, anger, and mistrust. Generally speaking, I made an ass of myself."

This time was completely different, even though the surgery was much more complicated, took twice as long, and in every way imaginable should have sent Doug over the edge.

Instead, on an early morning drive to the hospital, I was in prayer, and worship music played on the radio. While waiting for the surgical team to assemble, I knelt at my wife's bedside, took her hands in mine, and prayed out loud for her healing, for the surgical team, and for peace and comfort for both of us. Essentially, I told God what he already knew: *You're in charge. You have this. And I'm a wreck anyway, so I'm going to step out of the way and trust you with it.* All throughout the day, whenever a negative thought entered my mind, I gave it to God and returned to prayer.

Doug's wife needed ongoing support, which this time he was able to give.

Whenever my wife would start getting frustrated because she felt helpless, instead of my usual well-meaning but pointless response of trying to fix things, I would kneel by her bed, take her hand, and pray for both of us. I did everything I could throughout the day and night to make her burden lighter— everything from helping her position herself more comfortably to finding the TV remote every time it got lost in the seemingly endless hoses, tubes, and cords. In the end, the thing she needed most from me was a smile, brushing the hair from her face, and assurance that she was not a burden to me. Her greater needs of peace and comfort were not mine to give. Instead of being a wall and blocking God's gifts, I tried to become a window and let his peace and comfort shine through me.

His transformation hasn't been without its setbacks. For example, Doug let loose on his brother once, "who has a tendency to keep pushing when I've tried to remove myself from the situation. After the last incident, I apologized to him for losing my temper, but I explained to him that when I tell him to drop it, it means I'm feeling cornered. I asked him to respect that, at least temporarily. We are close, and for the most part we've been able to remain so despite my outbursts."

Killing his anger has given birth to other emotions and spiritual sensitivity and has essentially helped Doug become a whole person. "Anger is a funny thing. I can see now that it was my armor. It kept me from feeling all the other emotions that I might have felt. Hurt, helplessness, and disappointment were all rolled up under it. Without that armor, all of these feelings come through loud and clear."

Doug is learning to identify each emotion rather than smother everything with anger: *"What am I feeling? What is it rooted in? Is it from this circumstance or something from the past?* I take what I'm feeling and try to break it down. In the past, I struggled with grouping offenses together instead of dealing with them as they occurred. I have to break each one down now."

One of the greatest benefits to Doug's life in losing the toxicity was gaining friends. "To be honest, I didn't have a single true friend for twenty years. Now I have people I can talk to and with whom I can work through things."

Not surprisingly, adopting compassion and gentleness over anger has also transformed his marriage.

> I have a real marriage now. It has gradually improved, though there were some overnight changes that were more dramatic. We are much better at communicating with each other. I'm better at boundaries. I'm better at speaking out if I'm hurt, but not in a retaliatory way, so the problems get resolved instead of getting worse. Instead of talking *over* my wife, I talk *to* my wife. The difference in our marriage has been like night and day. Before, we were married in legal terms only. We weren't close. We didn't share our feelings. It was very much a roommate situation. We're very close friends now.

Work is still a difficult place for Doug to control his toxic behavior.

> As far as work goes, I still struggle. For the first time in thirty-five years, I took a job where I'm an equipment operator and a laborer. I have no responsibility for anything outside my labor. Control issues don't apply anymore, which helps me keep my anger in check. I don't have control, but I sleep at night, and I don't have the stress of worrying about how to make

things happen. I have reason to believe I'll soon be offered a supervisory role, but I'm not sure I'll accept it. It would be extremely challenging to me to be the person I know I should be and to take that position. I just know that right now I'm better off not being in charge—for me and my family. We're taking a financial hit, but for my welfare, that's the right thing to do right now.

Doug's marriage changed. His relationship with his brother changed. His work environment changed. Now even Doug's relationship to himself has changed. "I carried so much shame, but I'm not ashamed of who I am anymore. I made a decision that I'm not going to be that angry, toxic person anymore. Through Jesus, I realized I had a choice. I can respond to others how I want to. Jesus in me gives me that freedom. Of course, I've had some pretty spectacular fails, but they are few and far between, and I immediately go back and try to make amends."

Your toxicity may not seem as pronounced as Doug's. Maybe it's more sporadic. Maybe it's about control instead of hatred. But what was true for Doug is true for every one of us. Toxicity ruins everything about us and every relationship we have. Doug's life is proof that we don't have to give in to it. Because of Jesus we have a choice. We can put off anger, rage, malice, slander, and filthy language. Knowing we are chosen and dearly loved, we can put on compassion, kindness, humility, gentleness, and patience.

The first place to begin transforming a toxic world is to get rid of the toxicity in ourselves.

Takeaways

- Though it's toxic to control others, it's healthy to control ourselves. The first place to stop toxicity from spreading in this world is to keep it from emanating from us.
- The apostle Paul tells a new crop of Christians that faith in Jesus means getting rid of anger, rage, malice, slander, and filthy language

and putting on compassion, kindness, humility, gentleness, and patience.

- Transformation from anger to charity comes about not through willpower alone but through receiving the presence of Jesus into your life and letting his love and grace permeate your heart and mind. We act differently when we know we are chosen and dearly loved.
- Christians are most likely to act in a toxic way when they value being right over being like Christ. Scripture isn't a weapon to be used to hurt nonbelievers. Methods matter.
- Without excusing someone for their toxic behavior, learn how to have compassion for the "spiritual meningitis" that may have led to their condition. Get to know their backstory.
- Leaving toxic behavior behind transformed the way Doug relates to his wife, his children, his coworkers, and even himself.

CHAPTER 21

DON'T BE TOXIC
TO YOURSELF

Sofia had lived through an autumn filled with heartbreak and loss. Her best friend moved away. Her church fell apart. A work crisis demanded her attention for twelve hours a day, including weekends—which made her feel enormously guilty, since she's raising two young sons.

On January 1, when people make resolutions, Sofia decided to dust off her bathroom scale and survey the damage. "I'm a comfort food kind of person," she says. "When I feel stressed, food calms me down. I know it's not healthy, but sometimes you're just trying to get through the day."

She had been avoiding the scale because she knew the numbers wouldn't be good. So she wasn't especially surprised when her scale spit out three numbers in a combination she had never seen before. It was a slap to her face.

Sofia has a way with words. "My bathroom scale has no compassion, no understanding, and no empathy for how difficult my fall had been. Personally, I believe the scale should have cut me a break. It could have taken a few pounds off, knowing I had truly weathered a very difficult season and was already facing enormous guilt. But the scale was harsh. It said, 'You've got a lot of exercise and some much smaller meals in your immediate future. Oh, and forget about any pie or ice cream until at least Thanksgiving.'"

Our brains can be like Sofia's bathroom scale—cold, calculating, unfeeling, and unyielding. We can become our own worst enemies, pouring toxic thoughts into our neurological system in a way we never would do to anyone else. I was more concerned about the words coming out of Sofia's mouth than about the numbers on her scale:

"I'm so weak."

"I'm ashamed of myself."

"The other day I lashed out at my husband, but really, I was just having a bad day. And then I let fly against one of my daughters for accidentally making a mess. I went to bed thinking, *Sofia, are you sure you're even a Christian?*"

Do you ever, like Sofia, find yourself using toxic language *against yourself*? Maybe weight isn't your issue. But perhaps, like me, you've heard yourself saying, "I'm such an idiot." "How could I be so stupid?" "When will I ever grow up?"

Here's what I suggested to Sofia, and what I'm still struggling to apply to myself: *Anything you wouldn't say to someone else, stop saying to yourself.*

Isn't it true that some of us say things to ourselves we would *never* say to a friend or a child? As we bring this study to an end, let's talk a bit about being kind, not toxic, when you talk to *yourself*.

Francis de Sales counsels every lover of God, "As the mild and affectionate reproofs of a father have far greater power to reclaim his child than rage and passion; so when we have committed any fault, if we reprehend our heart with mild and calm [corrections], having more compassion for it than passion against it, sweetly encouraging it to amendment, the repentance it shall conceive by this means will sink much deeper, and penetrate it more effectually, than a fretful, injurious, and stormy repentance."[1]

God loves you. You're chosen and dearly loved! He hates it when toxic people attack you, *and* it stands to reason that he must hate it when you talk in a toxic way to yourself.

But what if we've really messed up? How do we avoid being toxic to ourselves when we are convinced we deserve it?

For me, toxic self-talk began to die when I realized what should have been so obvious—that Jesus, not me, is the hero in my life.

When I expect myself to be what only Jesus can be—perfectly loving, infinitely wise, supremely strong—I'm going to hate myself for falling so far short *every day*. When I accept that Jesus is my hero and will always be my hero, and that his life and grace are my only hope, when I spend more time thinking about his excellence than my pathetic weakness, toxic talk begins to die.

The Beauty That Consumes the Ugly

As I've already hinted, my language exceeds my experience in this regard. Though I now know that struggles and temptations make me more useful, I hate the humiliation they bring and regularly beat myself up for them. Yet the truth is that without them I'd probably be an insufferable, self-righteous monster who makes people feel guilty instead of inviting them to find refuge in the acceptance and grace of Jesus Christ.

There's a reason I'm so passionate about being "chosen and dearly loved" (Colossians 3:12). There's a reason I constantly remind myself that I'm called, loved, and kept (Jude 1). From this framework, I don't have to deny my sin. I don't pretend that God can begin to use me only when I "really" get my act together and stop doing that or start doing this. That's toxic. Instead, I'm thankful for Jesus.

When others get you down and attack you or when you begin attacking yourself, here's the place to run to—the beauty of Jesus, including both *who he is* and *what he's done*.

Turning to focus on the glory of Jesus has changed my life. I used to obsess over the toxic people who wounded me, but when I fretted about toxic people, I started to hate them. When I fretted about how weak and passive I can be, I hated myself. When I changed what I thought about, no longer thinking about toxic people or my own occasionally toxic self and started thinking about Jesus, it was like a miracle drug. Glorifying Jesus in your mind is that strong!

I'm now collecting celebrations of God throughout Scripture for my own use, but here are just a few I've gathered already from Colossians (using just one book of the Bible as an example). Imagine what could happen if you stopped worrying about someone who is hurting you, stopped thinking about how weak you are *again*, and started thinking about *this*:

- Jesus' grace (Colossians 1:6)
- that Jesus is the source of all wisdom and understanding (Colossians 1:9)
- Jesus' glorious might (Colossians 1:11)
- that God rescued us from the dominion of darkness and brought us into the kingdom of light (Colossians 1:13)
- that in Jesus all things were created (Colossians 1:16)
- that Jesus is before all things, and in him all things hold together (Colossians 1:17)
- that in everything Jesus has the supremacy (Colossians 1:18)
- that through Jesus, God has reconciled us to himself to present us as holy, without blemish, and free from accusation (Colossians 1:22)
- I delight that in Christ are hidden all the treasures of wisdom and knowledge (Colossians 2:3)
- that in Christ, God has made us alive (Colossians 2:13)
- lest I despair, I hold on to the fact that God forgave all our sins (Colossians 2:13), disarmed the powers and authorities of the world (Colossians 2:15), and testifies that he chose us and loves us dearly (Colossians 3:12)
- that Jesus is our peace (Colossians 3:15)
- that God is our Father (Colossians 3:17)

This is just one short excerpt out of just one short book in the Bible. There are hundreds of other pages to explore.

The best antidote for toxic self-talk is shunning the use of toxic language to berate yourself and instead nurturing your soul with healing words from Scripture. *Don't dwell on where you fail; dwell on where Christ excels.* His strength is greater than our weakness, so much greater, in fact, that talking about just a small portion of his magnificence changes the way we think, feel, and live. In a toxic world, meditating on Christ is like breathing pure oxygen.

Get off the mental bathroom scale and stop thinking about *yourself*; think about the purity and sufficiency of *Christ*. For me, this has become the foolproof way to stop being toxic to myself.

You will be best equipped to stand against the toxicity of the world when you understand that you matter, not because your earthly parents loved you and doted on you, or someone proposed to you or agreed to marry you, or a friend thinks you're the best friend ever, or your kids think you're the best parent in the world, but because God, the wisest and most perceptive Being in the universe, chose you and adopted you. We all need to live by the truth of Colossians 3:12—that we are "chosen and dearly loved." When you consider that the source of our acceptance and love is none other than the God of the universe, lesser opinions cease to matter. What do I care if the rest of the world rejects me when the most brilliant Being alive—God himself—not only chooses me but loves me dearly?

Let this be your daily theme song: "chosen and dearly loved." Sing it to yourself in the morning; hum it to yourself during the day—"chosen and dearly loved." Thank God for it in the evening: "I'm chosen and dearly loved!"

Bask in God's acceptance and delight. You can't make everyone like you; in this toxic world, it is certain that everyone *won't* like you. So put your identity in the One who loves you dearly, who says, "I chose you and will keep choosing you." Your best defense against toxic people's rejection is your holy Father's acceptance. Your best shield from the world's animosity is the Creator's passionate pursuit.

You don't have to defend yourself. You don't have to engage your enemies. Simply lift up your hands and be loved. Embrace your mission and walk away with Jesus from anyone who seeks to stop you from doing what God has called you to do or from being the person God has called you to be.

God's grace, God's beauty, God's acceptance, and God's affirmation are the most powerful antidotes against the toxicity found in this fallen world. Let's all choose to live out of his affirmation.

Spiritual Health

Sofia lost ten pounds by May but gained five back over a difficult summer. She realized that feeling bad about herself and shaming herself didn't make her a better mother or wife. It didn't actually help her lose weight, and it certainly didn't please God.

She took Francis de Sales's words to heart and focused on speaking *gently* to herself, a simple concept that breathed life into her soul. And then she started intentionally encouraging herself. "You had a good day, Sofia. When Martina accidentally dropped her bowl, your first thought was to calm her, not lash out at her. And did you see the way she looked at you? That was a nice moment. That's what she's going to remember years from now."

I didn't give Sofia "ten steps to stop being toxic to yourself." I just presented the issue from a pastoral perspective. "How does God want you to talk to you?"

That was enough for Sofia. She stopped the self-talk based on anger, rage, malice, slander, and filthy language and instead started speaking to herself with compassion, kindness, gentleness, and patience. *If that's how God wants us to treat others*, she reasoned, *isn't it how he'd want us to treat ourselves?*

Guess what? By learning to treat herself more kindly, Sofia has started treating others more kindly as well. Toxic behavior, even when it's directed at ourselves, tends to spread. Spiritual health does too. Sofia has chosen spiritual health, and it has made a world of difference.

Let's stop being toxic toward anyone, *including ourselves*. Make Jesus your hero, find your refuge in him, and begin making this world a much healthier place.

Takeaways

- If God hates it when others treat us in a toxic manner, it stands to reason that he hates it when we treat ourselves in a toxic manner.
- Anything we wouldn't say to someone else is something we shouldn't say to ourselves.

- Toxic self-talk begins to die when we make Jesus our hero and stop expecting so much from ourselves.
- Spiritual health is built on meditating on the excellence of Christ more than we think about the toxicity of others or our own weaknesses.
- Sofia's toxic self-talk was transformed by learning to be gentler with herself and to stop talking to herself with anger, rage, malice, slander, and filthy language and instead to start speaking to herself with compassion, kindness, gentleness, and patience.

EPILOGUE

As I drew near to the end of the writing of this book, I woke up with a vivid dream. I don't usually talk about such dreams, as people are understandably suspicious of them, which is why I've saved this for the epilogue. You've seen the many Scriptures I've relied on and set these truths in, but sometimes God chooses to speak to me in the early morning hours when my mind doesn't have as many guards or prejudices up. A dream followed by a long stream of understanding doesn't happen often in my life, but when it does, it can cleanse my soul and open up wide avenues of new understanding, which I always test with Scripture.

In the dream, I was being viciously bullied. I couldn't tell how old I was or where I was, but I could *feel* the bullying experience. When I awoke, God led me on a journey through my life, where I saw episode after episode of being bullied. Before that morning, if you had asked me if I had been bullied, I would have immediately said, "No, not really." But God helped me revisit many episodes with many toxic people throughout my life. There were a few blessed bully-free seasons in my life, but I was astonished at how many toxic episodes I had forgotten about—and how they had hurt me and shaped me and caused me to doubt and limit myself.

Later that very same day, I faced yet another bully. By God's grace I felt spiritually, intellectually, and emotionally prepared. It didn't impact me like it could have or would have in the past. It almost made me laugh as I sensed that God had prepared me so well.

The apostle Paul's view of Christianity has to do with God the Father setting the world to rights through Jesus and his Holy Spirit. God will finish the task when the new heaven and the new earth are joined in eternity, but in the meantime, in the land of what theologians call "the already but not yet," God is setting the world to rights by inspiring his followers to do imperfectly what he will one day finish perfectly.

Bullies should take notice. The church has been warned, armed, and released against bullies' controlling, murderous, and toxic ways. God has them in his sights. He has said, "Enough is enough," and their days are numbered. God will deal with toxic bullies in the future, but I believe he also wants to lessen their impact *today*.

Through *you*.

In the meantime, build your *offense*. Study God's Word, pray, surrender to God in obedience and direction, learn what it means to be filled with and guided by the Holy Spirit, seek first the kingdom of God in all things, and invest generously and enthusiastically in the lives of reliable people who are qualified to teach others.

And when necessary, don't be afraid to play *defense*. Understand what a toxic opponent looks like, smells like, talks like, and acts like. When the situation calls for it, follow in the footsteps of Jesus and walk away from the toxicity and toward a healthy life, a pure mind, focused service, and genuine love.

Choose to walk away and find *freedom* in Christ.

ACKNOWLEDGMENTS

First, I'd like to thank the numerous people who allowed their stories of God's healing and protection to be shared so that others could be blessed. Some wanted their names changed and identifying details altered, but I am grateful for each of them. Their stories provide a rich context for understanding the truths taken from Scripture.

Many people generously read earlier incarnations of this manuscript and offered helpful critiques, for which I'm very grateful. These include Lisa Thomas, Andi Perkins, Darin Slack, Deb Fileta, Kevin Harney, Ella Hutchinson, Mike Woodruff, Eric Spath (who was the first and most ardent backer of this book, telling me after I did a talk on toxic people, "This *has* to be your next book"), Sheila Gregoire, David and Megan Cox, Dr. Steve Wilke, Brad Hambrick, Mary Kay Smith (who has reviewed every manuscript I've written, prepublication, since *Sacred Pathways* came out in 1996), Dr. Mitch Whitman, and Bob Kellemen. They all reviewed earlier drafts, and many or all may disagree with some of my final conclusions.

My assistant at Second Baptist, Alli Sepulveda, is enormously helpful, protecting my pockets of writing time, moving this ministry forward, and keeping my schedule in order when I'm traveling. Toni Richmond, a colleague here at Second, heard me give an evening sermon on toxic people and became an enthusiastic supporter of my speaking out on this topic, making me think more might need to be said. I am deeply grateful for the generous support and fellowship that Lisa and I enjoy at Second Baptist as writer-in-residence, under the leadership of Dr. Ed Young. Being on the teaching team and getting involved in the life of an urban church have proved to be such a blessing.

I owe a big debt to my agents, Curtis Yates and Mike Salisbury. Mike championed this as my next book when I was reluctant, and his encouragement is what kept the idea alive and then pushed it over the edge. If I'm counting correctly, this marks the fourteenth book that Yates and Yates have represented for me. True partners all the way.

This was my first opportunity to work with Andy Rogers, a young editor at Zondervan who was fabulous with his suggestions for needed stories, cutting extraneous material (you've been spared many archaic quotes from my beloved Christian classics), and refining the message you now hold in your hands.

David Morris at Zondervan and his encouraging support remind me of the "glory days" of working with Scott Bolinder (who championed *Sacred Marriage*). David has been so welcoming and helpful and makes me deeply grateful to have my publishing "home" with Zondervan.

Many thanks to Tom Dean and Brandon Henderson of the marketing team and Dirk Buursma of the editing team. I pray Dirk doesn't retire until after I do, as it would be a much different experience to release a book that hasn't gone through his very capable editing hands.

JESUS WALKING AWAY

These are the biblical accounts I found where Jesus chose to walk away or let someone else walk away.

> When Jesus saw the crowd around him, he gave orders to cross to the other side of the lake.
>
> MATTHEW 8:18

> Then the whole town went out to meet Jesus. And when they saw him, they pleaded with him to leave their region. Jesus stepped into a boat, crossed over and came to his own town.
>
> MATTHEW 8:34–9:1

> But they laughed at [Jesus]. *After the crowd had been put outside*, he went in and took the girl by the hand, and she got up.
>
> MATTHEW 9:24–25, EMPHASIS ADDED

> But the Pharisees went out and plotted how they might kill Jesus. Aware of this, Jesus withdrew from that place.
>
> MATTHEW 12:14–15

> When Jesus heard what had happened, he withdrew by boat privately to a solitary place.
>
> MATTHEW 14:13

Immediately Jesus made the disciples get into the boat and go on ahead of him to the other side, while he dismissed the crowd. After he had dismissed them, he went up on a mountainside by himself to pray.

MATTHEW 14:22

After Jesus had sent the crowd away, he got into the boat and went to the vicinity of Magadan.

MATTHEW 15:39

"A wicked and adulterous generation looks for a sign, but none will be given it except the sign of Jonah." Jesus then left them and went away.

MATTHEW 16:4

In this passage where Jesus encounters a rich young man (Matthew 19:16–30), Jesus lets him walk away. Instead of chasing after him, he turns to his disciples and teaches them.

When the young man heard this [the teaching to sell all that he owned], he went away sad, because he had great wealth.

MATTHEW 19:22

But when the chief priests and the teachers of the law saw . . . they were indignant. "Do you hear what these children are saying?" they asked him. "Yes," replied Jesus, "have you never read, 'From the lips of children and infants you, Lord, have called forth your praise'?" And he left them and went out of the city to Bethany, where he spent the night.

MATTHEW 21:15–17

When [the Pharisees] heard this [Jesus avoiding their trap], they were amazed. So they left him and went away.

MATTHEW 22:22

Jesus excoriated the Pharisees with the seven woes (Matthew 23:13–39), after which he walked away.

Jesus left the temple and was walking away when his disciples came up to him to call his attention to its buildings.

MATTHEW 24:1

When they found him, they exclaimed: "Everyone is looking for you!" Jesus replied, "Let us go somewhere else—to the nearby villages—so I can preach there also. That is why I have come."

MARK 1:37–38

Jesus sent [the man with leprosy] away at once with a strong warning.

MARK 1:43

That day when evening came, he said to his disciples, "Let us go over to the other side." Leaving the crowd behind, they took him along, just as he was, in the boat.

MARK 4:35–36

Then the people began to plead with Jesus to leave their region. As Jesus was getting into the boat the man who had been demon-possessed begged to go with him. Jesus did not let him.

MARK 5:17–19

He did not let anyone follow him except Peter, James and John the brother of James.

MARK 5:37

But they laughed at him. After [Jesus] put them all out, he took the child's father and mother and the disciples who were with him, and went in where the child was.

MARK 5:40

Immediately Jesus made his disciples get into the boat and go on ahead of him to Bethsaida, while he dismissed the crowd. After leaving them, he went up on a mountainside to pray.

MARK 6:45–46

Jesus left that place and went to the vicinity of Tyre. He entered a house and did not want anyone to know it.

MARK 7:24

The Pharisees came and began to question Jesus. To test him, they asked him for a sign from heaven. He sighed deeply and said, "Why does this generation ask for a sign? Truly I tell you, no sign will be given to it." Then he left them, got back into the boat and crossed to the other side.

MARK 8:11–13

Jesus looked at him and loved him. "One thing you lack," he said. "Go, sell everything you have and give to the poor, and you will have treasure in heaven. Then come, follow me." At this the man's face fell. He went away sad, because he had great wealth. Jesus looked around and said to his disciples, "How hard it is for the rich to enter the kingdom of God!"

MARK 10:21–24

On reaching Jerusalem, Jesus entered the temple courts and began driving out those who were buying and selling there.

MARK 11:15

But [the chief priests, the teachers of the law and the elders] were afraid of the crowd; so they left him and went away.

MARK 12:12

The chief priests accused [Jesus] of many things. So again Pilate asked him, "Aren't you going to answer? See how many things they are accusing you of." But Jesus still made no reply, and Pilate was amazed.

Mark 15:3–5

When the devil had finished all this tempting, he left him until an opportune time.

Luke 4:13

All the people in the synagogue were furious when they heard this. They got up, drove him out of the town, and took him to the brow of the hill on which the town was built, in order to throw him off the cliff. But he walked right through the crowd and went on his way.

Luke 4:28–30

At daybreak, Jesus went out to a solitary place. The people were looking for him and when they came to where he was, they tried to keep him from leaving them. But he said, "I must proclaim the good news of the kingdom of God to the other towns also, because that is why I was sent." And he kept on preaching in the synagogues of Judea.

Luke 4:42–44

Yet the news about him spread all the more, so that crowds of people came to hear him and to be healed of their sicknesses. But Jesus often withdrew to lonely places and prayed.

Luke 5:15–16

Then all the people of the region of the Gerasenes asked Jesus to leave them, because they were overcome with fear. So he got into the boat and left.

Luke 8:37

The man from whom the demons had gone out begged to go with him, but Jesus sent him away, saying, "Return home and tell how much God has done for you." So the man went away and told all over town how much Jesus had done for him.

LUKE 8:38–39

As the time approached for him to be taken up to heaven, Jesus resolutely set out for Jerusalem. And he sent messengers on ahead, who went into a Samaritan village to get things ready for him; but the people there did not welcome him, because he was heading for Jerusalem . . . Then he and his disciples went to another village.

LUKE 9:51–53, 56

In this passage (John 5:1–15), Jesus slips away from the Pharisees before they can question him about telling a healed man to carry his mat away.

The man who was healed had no idea who it was [that had healed him], for Jesus had slipped away into the crowd that was there.

JOHN 5:13

Jesus, knowing that they intended to come and make him king by force, withdrew again to a mountain by himself.

JOHN 6:15

From this time many of his disciples turned back and no longer followed him. "You do not want to leave too, do you?" Jesus asked the Twelve.

JOHN 6:66–67

After this, Jesus went around in Galilee. He did not want to go about in Judea because the Jewish leaders there were looking for a way to kill him.

JOHN 7:1

At this, they picked up stones to stone him, but Jesus hid himself, slipping away from the temple grounds.

JOHN 8:59

Again [Jesus' opponents] tried to seize him, but he escaped their grasp. Then Jesus went back across the Jordan to the place where John had been baptizing in the early days.

JOHN 10:39–40

So from that day on they plotted to take his life. Therefore Jesus no longer moved about publicly among the people of Judea. Instead he withdrew to a region near the wilderness, to a village called Ephraim, where he stayed with his disciples.

JOHN 11:53–54

When he had finished speaking, Jesus left and hid himself from them.

JOHN 12:36

As soon as Judas took the bread, Satan entered into him. So Jesus told him, "What you are about to do, do quickly." But no one at the meal understood why Jesus said this to him. Since Judas had charge of the money, some thought Jesus was telling him to buy what was needed for the festival, or to give something to the poor. As soon as Judas had taken the bread, he went out. And it was night. When he was gone, Jesus said, "Now is the Son of Man glorified and God is glorified in him."

JOHN 13:27–31

NOTES

Chapter 1: A Most Clever Attack

1. John Climacus, *The Ladder of Divine Ascent*, trans. Colm Luibheid and Norman Russell (New York: Paulist, 1982), 149.

Chapter 2: Walkaway Jesus

1. The same Jesus who said "turn the other cheek" also told his disciples to buy a sword (Luke 22:36). The same Jesus who said he was "gentle" (Matthew 11:29) forcefully chased the money changers out of the temple, using a whip (John 2:15). In Matthew 5:22, Jesus says that calling someone a fool puts you in danger of the fires of hell; in Matthew 23:17, Jesus calls the Pharisees and teachers of the law "blind fools." We have to read Jesus' words in context and with the proper weight, in the same way that we understand his "gouge out your eyes rather than lust" comment as a metaphor of sin's seriousness, not as a directive for someone to actually follow. Trying to avoid a *pattern* of Jesus' behavior and teaching with one outlier comment should cause us to look at the outlier comment with a more precise understanding.

Chapter 3: A Murderous Spirit

1. M. Scott Peck, *People of the Lie: The Hope for Healing Human Evil* (1983; repr., New York: Touchstone, 1998, 73.

2. Peck, *People of the Lie*, 255.

Chapter 4: Control Mongers

1. C. S. Lewis, *The Screwtape Letters* (1942: repr., New York: Bantam, 1995), 53.

2. John Calvin, *The Bondage and Liberation of the Will: A Defence of the Orthodox Doctrine of Human Choice against Pighius* (Grand Rapids: Baker, 1996), 69.
3. Calvin, *Bondage and Liberation of the Will*, 69–70.
4. Jack Deere, *Even in Our Darkness: A Story of Beauty in a Broken Life* (Grand Rapids: Zondervan, 2018), 244.

Chapter 5: Loving Hate

1. Dan Allender and Tremper Longman III, *Bold Love* (Colorado Springs: NavPress, 1992), 237.
2. Dr. Henry Cloud and Dr. John Townsend, *Boundaries: When to Say Yes, How to Say No to Take Control of Your Life* (1992; repr., Grand Rapids: Zondervan, 2017), 98.
3. Francis de Sales, *Introduction to the Devout Life* (London: Aeterna, 2015), 127.
4. De Sales, *Introduction to the Devout Life*, 129.
5. De Sales, *Introduction to the Devout Life*, 129.
6. Personal correspondence with Brad, in reaction to reading an earlier version of this manuscript.

Chapter 6: No Time to Waste

1. Andrew Murray, *Like Christ: Thoughts on the Blessed Life of Conformity to the Son of God* (London: Nisbet, 1884), 81–82, italics original.
2. Quoted in Francis B. Carpenter, *The Inner Life of Abraham Lincoln: Six Months at the White House* (Lincoln: University of Nebraska Press, 1995), 258–59.
3. Aldous Huxley, *The Devils of Loudun* (New York: HarperCollins, 1952), 192, 260.

Chapter 7: Reliable People

1. John Climacus, *The Ladder of Divine Ascent*, trans. Colm Luibheid and Norman Russell (New York: Paulist, 1982), 246.
2. Information taken from Rosaria Butterfield's website (www.rosaria butterfield.com/biography).
3. Rosaria Champagne Butterfield, *The Secret Thoughts of an Unlikely Convert: An English Professor's Journey into Christian Faith* (Pittsburgh, PA: Crown & Covenant, 2012), 8.

4. Butterfield, *Secret Thoughts of an Unlikely Convert*, 9.

5. Butterfield, *Secret Thoughts of an Unlikely Convert*, 10.

6. Butterfield, *Secret Thoughts of an Unlikely Convert*, 11.

7. Rosaria Butterfield, *The Gospel Comes with a House Key: Practicing Radically Ordinary Hospitality in Our Post-Christian World* (Wheaton, IL: Crossway, 2018).

8. "A GenRef Podcast: Interview with Rosaria Butterfield and Ken Smith," March 12, 2013, https://gentlereformation.com/2013/03/12/a-genref-podcast-interview-with-rosaria-butterfield-ken-smith.

Chapter 8: Pigs and Pearls

1. Dr. Henry Cloud and Dr. John Townsend, *Boundaries: When to Say Yes, How to Say No to Take Control of Your Life* (1992; repr., Grand Rapids: Zondervan, 2017), 86.

2. Cloud and Townsend, *Boundaries*, 88.

3. Dan Allender and Tremper Longman III, *Bold Love* (Colorado Springs: NavPress, 1992), 243.

Chapter 9: Love Tells the Truth

1. Leslie Vernick, *The Emotionally Destructive Marriage: How to Find Your Voice and Reclaim Your Hope* (Colorado Springs: WaterBrook, 2013).

2. Louis of Granada, *The Sinner's Guide* (London: Aeterna, 2015), 221.

3. Granada, *Sinner's Guide*, 222.

4. Granada, *Sinner's Guide*, 222.

5. Francis de Sales, *Introduction to the Devout Life* (London: Aeterna, 2015), 133–34.

6. Personal conversation with Dr. Wilke, April 18, 2018.

Chapter 10: A Man with a Mission

1. John Climacus, *The Ladder of Divine Ascent*, trans. Colm Luibheid and Norman Russell (New York: Paulist, 1982), 146.

Chapter 12: Learning How to Be Hated

1. George Whitefield, "Persecution: Every Christian's Lot," www.blueletterbible.org/Comm/whitefield_george/Sermons/witf_055.cfm.

2. Francis de Sales, *Introduction to the Devout Life* (London: Aeterna, 2015), 160.

3. Thomas Carroll, ed., *Jeremy Taylor: Selected Works* (New York: Paulist, 1990), 364.

4. Personal email sent by Sheila Wray Gregoire to me, May 8, 2018. Used with permission.

5. These five points come from a personal email sent by Kevin Harney to me on May 6, 2018. Used with permission.

6. John Climacus, *The Ladder of Divine Ascent*, trans. Colm Luibheid and Norman Russell (New York: Paulist, 1982), 149.

7. Climacus, *Ladder of Divine Ascent*, 149.

8. Climacus, *Ladder of Divine Ascent*, 149.

9. Climacus, *Ladder of Divine Ascent*, 117–18; the last sentence after the ellipses actually looks back and is pulled from page 115.

10. Climacus, *Ladder of Divine Ascent*, 149.

Chapter 13: Scripture's Skeleton

1. Dallas Willard, *Renovation of the Heart: Putting on the Character of Christ* (Colorado Springs: NavPress, 2002), 46.

2. N. T. Wright, *Romans*, in *The New Interpreter's Bible*, vol. X (Nashville: Abingdon, 2002), 767.

3. Jonathan Leeman, *How the Nations Rage: Rethinking Faith and Politics in a Divided Age* (Nashville: Nelson, 2018), 100, italics original.

4. Quoted in Philip Norman, *Paul McCartney: The Life* (New York: Little, Brown and Company, 2016), 223.

5. Norman, *Paul McCartney*, 222–23.

Chapter 14: A New Allegiance

1. Jack Deere, *Even in Our Darkness: A Story of Beauty in a Broken Life* (Grand Rapids: Zondervan, 2018), 210.

2. Robert J. Morgan, *The Red Sea Rules: 10 God-Given Strategies for Difficult Times* (Nashville: W. Publishing, 2014), 83, italics original.

Chapter 16: Toxic Parents

1. G. K. Chesterton, *Robert Browning* (London, 1903), 80, 73.

2. Chesterton, *Robert Browning*, 74.

3. Alvaro de Silva, ed., *Brave New Family: G. K. Chesterton on Men and Women, Children, Sex, Divorce, Marriage and the Family* (San Francisco: Ignatius, 1990), 20.

4. De Silva, *Brave New Family*, 20.

5. M. Scott Peck, *People of the Lie: The Hope for Healing Human Evil* (1983; repr., New York: Touchstone, 1998), 130.

6. Peck, *People of the Lie*, 51–52.

7. Peck, *People of the Lie*, 56.

Chapter 17: Toxic Marriages

1. M. Scott Peck, *People of the Lie: The Hope for Healing Human Evil* (1983; repr., New York: Touchstone, 1998), 76–77 (footnote).

Chapter 19: Toxic Children

1. Personal conversation with Dr. Wilke.

Chapter 20: Trading Toxic for Tender

1. Richard Rohr, "The Rent You Pay for Being Here," Richard Rohr's Daily Meditations, August 1, 2013, http://conta.cc/1aY7HeA, italics original.

Chapter 21: Don't Be Toxic to Yourself

1. Francis de Sales, *Introduction to the Devout Life* (London: Aeterna, 2015), 91.

New Video Study for Your Church or Small Group

If you've enjoyed this book, now you can go deeper with the companion video Bible study!

In this six-session study, Gary Thomas helps you apply the principles in *When to Walk Away* to your life. The study guide includes video notes, group discussion questions, and personal study and reflection materials for in-between sessions.

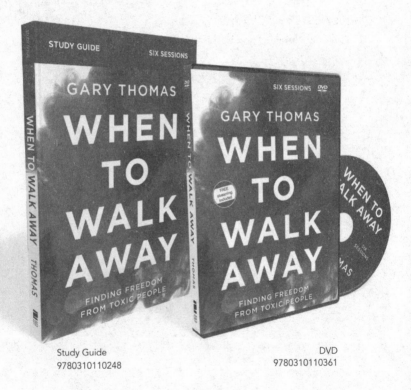

Study Guide
9780310110248

DVD
9780310110361

Available now at your favorite bookstore, or streaming video on StudyGateway.com.